ספר חפץ חיים

sefer

CHOFETZ CHAIM

ספר חפץ חיים

sefer

CHOFETZ CHAIM

with the commentary
YAD DOVID

by Rabbi Dovid Marchant

VOLUME ONE
The Foreword and
the first chapter of
Rabbi Yisroel Meir Kagan's
classic guide to the
laws of forbidden speech,
with full English translation
and an extensive overview
of the basic concepts

FELDHEIM PUBLISHERS
JERUSALEM · NEW YORK

ISBN-0-87306-845-9

   Rabbi Dovid Marchant
   12 Ezras Torah
   Jerusalem 95320

Edited by: R. Shlomo Fox-Ashrei

Feldheim Publishers
POB 35002
Jerusalem, Israel

Feldheim Publishers
200 Airport Executive Park
Nanuet, NY 10954

Printed in Israel

Rabbi CHAIM P. SCHEINBERG
Rosh Hayeshiva "TORAH-ORE"
and Morah Hora'ah of Kiryat Mattersdorf

הרב חיים פינחס שיינברג
ראש ישיבת "תורה-אור"
ומורה הוראה דקרית מטרסדורף

מכתב תהלה

הנני בזה ממלא רצונו הטהור של האברך היקר והנעלה אשר יראת
ה' אוצרו ה"ה ר' דוד מרצינ'ט שליט"א וכבר נודע שמו בישראל מספריו
הראשונים הבנה בשמיטה (אנגלית) והשאיפה לגדלות, והראה לי עלים
מספרו החדש שהוא תרגום אנגלי לספר הקדוש והנפלא חפץ חיים
הלכות לשון הרע ורכילות, ותרגומו כולל ביאור רחב וצלול על כל פרט
ופרט **בין במקור החיים ובין בבאר מים חיים** והדברים ניכרים היטב
שיגע ועמל מאד בעמלה של תורה לברר הסוגיות המובאות בבמ"ח
ודברי החח"ח זצ"ל שדן ופלפל בהן. וגם הרבה מאד בקנייני התורה
ובפרט בדיבוק חברים והרבה נשא ונתן עם בקיאים מופלגים מבינים
בעניינים אלו. ועוד בהיותו בק"ק דגייטסהעד זכה למסור שיעורים
לבני תורה בהל' לשה"ר ובספר ח"ח. והספר הזה דבר נחוץ מאד
בזמנינו במיוחד. ואמרו רז"ל ביומא ט: שמשום שנאת חנם נחרב הבית
וגלינו מארצינו וביאר החח"ח זצ"ל בהקדמתו שהכוונה בזה ללשון הרע
ג"כ שהיוצאת מצד השנאה דאי לאו הכי לא היו נענשים כ"כ ועיי"ש,
וכל כמה שלא נראה לתקן זה החטא איך תוכל להיות הגאולה וכמו
שהרחיב שם בענין זה החח"ח הקדוש. וג"כ שראינו בזמנינו התעוררות
גדולה בהלכות אלו ולכן אפריון נמטייה להרה"ג הנ"ל שקבל על עצמו
עבודת הקודש הזאת, מלאכת שמים וזכה לסייעתא דשמיא לחבר ספר
זה. ושמחתי מאד לראות פרי רוח ועמלו לזכות לדוברי אנגלית
בלימוד הנפלא הזה. ודבר גדול עשה בזה שפתח הסתום לאנשים אלו
הצמאים ללמוד ולהבין דברי קדשו של החח"ח זצ"ל וספרו היסודי
והעיקרי הזה, וערך כשלחן ערוך לפניהם בלשון ברור וקל. ובוודאי
יביא תועלת רבה לדעת הלכה למעשה בעניני לשה"ר וכו' וחובה
מוטלת על כאו"א ללמוד הלכות אלו שכמעט א"א להנצל ממכשול
בעניינים אלו בלי לימוד בקביעות בהם. על כן אמינא לפעלא טבא יישר
כוחו שחפץ ה' בידו יצליח וכל המזכה הרבים זכות הרבים תלוי בו,
ונזכה כולנו שיתקיים הבטחת הנביא ומלאה הארץ דיעה את ה' וכו'
בביאת גוא"צ בב"א. היום ו' אדר התשנ"ד ירושלים

הכותב והחותם למען התורה ולומדיה

רחוב פנים מאירות 2, ירושלים, ת. ד. 6979, טל. 371513-(02), ישראל
2, Panim Meirot St., Jerusalem, P. O. B. 6 9 7 9, Tel (02)-371513, Israel

RABBI MOISHE STERNBUCH

Vice President "Eda Hacharedis"
And Dayan Jerusalem Beth-Din
Head Torah Centre Community
Johannesburg S.A.

S.A. Address: 63 Fortesque Rd.
Yeoville Johannesburg
Tel: 271-1-648-5374   Fax: 271-1-648-5456

משה שטרנבוך

סגן נשיא העדה החרדית בעיה"ק

מח"ס "מועדים וזמנים", שו"ת "תשובות והנהגות" ועוד

ראב"ד דק"ק חרדים ביוהנסבורג

הכתובת בירושלים:

רח' משקלוב 13, הר-נוף, ירושלים

טל: 511780   פקס: 519610

בעזהי"ת, יום ___ אדר א' אאמל חפ"ג

אדונינו הרב המופלג ו ואוולו לשם ואהלה ונודע וצדיק פסט"ר הגדול ליברת גוב אולקינו שליט"א

ולאני סברו דל דלואמ לאון לנות הרצ, צ"ב נסע הרבות "הפל מ"ק, וריאר ינורים ל"ב נוב, והיל

שלאון לם וכל דלואן אנל"ית השמונו, ונגר סלוסו לאון הרל שנפשמורין, ענל נדן דואונ

כולנת כולאם ל'לגר, וזצ'ר דפסו לתם עיר אצוגד' אנגל"ית האנג' הל בת אולי ולאגן לגרי

...

ונעל: שלנד, כלאון ל'רחון פענק אריום

הרה"ג ר' משה שטרנבוך שליט"א
סגן נשיא העדה החרדית בעיה"ק
וראב"ד דק"ק חרדים ביוהנסבורג

בעזהי"ת יום ער"ח תמוז תשנ"ז

לכבוד הרב המופלא ומופלג לשם ותהלה ונודע בשעריו בספריו היקרים
ה"ה הרב דוד מרצ'נט שליט"א

קבלתי ספרו על הלכות לשון הרע, ע"פ הספר הקדוש "חפץ חיים", וביאר
הדברים ב"יד דוד", והכל בלשון צח וקל בלשון אנגלית המדובר, וידוע
שאיסור לשון הרע מהחמורות, ואך ורק בלימוד ההלכות יכולים ליזהר,
ועכשיו בספרו פתח שער לדוברי אנגלית ללמוד הלכות אלו ולהבין גדרי
האיסור.

ועיקר התיקון ללשון הרע שיקדש מעכשיו דיבורו, וע"כ אפילו עד עכשיו לא
נזהר הדלת פתוח לו, ודוקא באיסור הפרוץ מאד ואדם מקדש עצמו ליזהר
שכרו על זה יותר, וסיפר לי מו"ר הגר"מ שניידער זצ"ל ששמע ששאלו החח"
זצ"ל עצמו למה הוא לא מביא ומדגיש דברי הרמב"ם בהלכות תשובה (פ"ג ה"ה).
"ואלו הן שאין להם חלק לעולם הבא אלא נכרתים ואובדנין ונידונין על גודל
רשעם וחטאתם לעולם ולעולמי עולמים המינים והאפיקורסים והכופרים
בתורה והכופרים בתחיית המתים ובביאת הגואל וכו' ושופכי דמים ובעלי
לשון הרע והמושך ערלתו." הרי שמספרי לשון הרע דינם כמינים
ואפיקורסים ורוצחים שנידונים לעולם ועד? והשיב החח" זצ"ל "פצצה כזאת
לא רציתי להשליך", ופירש כוונתו שאם ידמו שדינו כאפיקורס ונידון לעולם,
ידמה שאין לו תיקון ולא יחזור בתשובה, וע"כ בחר להשמיטו, והאמת שיש
לזה תיקון, והיינו כשמקבל ע"ע ונזהר כראוי מכאן ולהבא (ובפ"ז דדיעות
שהמסבר לה"ר ככופר בעיקר ע"ש). וחלק גדול בעם ישראל שמדברים
אנגלית ימצאו בספרו בלשון הדינים, וכפי שעיינתי שוה לכל נפש, וגם בני תורה
ימצאו בלשון צח וקל על הדברים וההלכות, ונקוה
בס"ד שיקבעו בספרו שיעורים ובחינות בבתי חינוך שעם חינוך בנוער קל
יותר ליזהר, וחובת חינוך לכל המצוות ואסורים וכ"ש ליזהר מלה"ר
ורכילות.

והנה חז"ל אמרו תלמוד מביא לידי מעשה ובית קדשינו חרב מפני שנאת
חנם המקור ללשון הרע וכשמתקנים השורש ימהר הקב"ה ויחיש גאולתינו,
וכשהפקר אצל אדם איסור לשון הרע אמרו חז"ל שאיסור לגור אצלו כשכן
(עיין רמב"ם פ"ז דיעות ה"ו), ובתיקונו עושה שלום למעלה ולמטה, ולכן
בשמחה אני מצרף ברכתי שהספר יתפשט ויתהדר בבית ישראל וימהר
הקב"ה ויחיש גאולתינו ופדות נפשינו
והנני מצפה בכליון לרחמי שמים מרובים.

משה שטרנבוך

RABBI B. RAKOW
Rav of Gateshead
138 Whitehall Road,
Gateshead NE8 1TP
Tyne & Wear
☎ (0191) 477 3012

בצלאל בהרה"ח ג"ר' יום טוב ליפמאן ראקאוו

אב"ד דגייטסהעד

ב"ה יו׳ ...

כבוד ידיד"נ הרב הגאון וכו׳ וכו׳ וכו׳ שליט"א

...

ב"ה י"ד תמוז תשנ"ז לפ"ק

כבוד ידידנו הרב המופלג וגדול בתורה ויראת שמים הרב דוד מרצ'נט
שליט"א שלח אלי עלים מספרו מקור החיים (ובאר מים חיים) באנגלית עם
ביאורו יד דוד שרוצה להוציא לאור לזכות את הרבים ולהצילם מהעון
החמור של לשון הרע.

באמת כבר ידוע ואין להאריך בגודל הנחיצות לספרים כאלו. רק רצוני להעיד
על המחבר שליט"א אחרי שידיעתי את גודל העמל והיגיעה שהשקיע
בלימוד ספרי החפץ חיים ושעליו אפשר לומר נאה דורש ונאה מקיים.

כבר ידוע שהחפץ חיים זצוקלללה"ה קיבל הסכמה על ספרו שמירת הלשון
מאת הגאון האדיר מגדולי הדור דאז מהו"ר בן ציון בילסקר זצ"ל רק אחרי
שבדק אחריו כשבוע ימים אם זה המחבר נאה דורש וגם נאה מקיים.

לזה הנני לאחל לכ' ידידנו המחבר שיזכה לברך על המוגמר להוציא ספרו
לאור עולם ולזכות בזה את הרבים.

ובזכות זה נזכה לגאולה שלימה בקרוב.

הכותב וחותם לכ' עמלים בתורה ולכ' המחבר שליט"א

הקט' בצלאל ראקאוו

ישיבה דפילאדעלפיא
בס"ד

בס"ד יום עלינו גמלך

לכבוד הרב הגאון וכו' דורש שלום

ולברכה לי' ספרי ר' דוד ארזי שליט"א

אחרי דרישת שלום והברכה כראוי.

הנני לציין הגדיני מסרו הספר החדש וכו' ...
...
...
...
...

...

דברי הכותב וחותם לכבוד התורה

[חתימה]

בס"ד ב' אלול תשנ"ז

למע"כ הרב המופלג נודע בשערים לשם ולתהלה ע"י ספריו
ר' דוד מרצ'נט, שליט"א

אחרי מבוא השלום והברכה כראוי,

העלים לדוגמא הגיעני מספרו החשוב תרגום בשפת אנגלית ספר
חפץ חיים וכלול בתרגומו המקור החיים ובאר מים חיים בהרחבה
וביאורים נפלאים שוה לכל נפש. כנראה ששקע כבודו יגיעה רבה
ועמלות רב להוציא מרגניתא טבא וללבן ולברר כמה עניינים. רוב
הדברים כבר ערכו כור הבחינה שנאמרו בשיעורים לרבים ובפני
תלמידי חכמים.

למותר לדבר על חומר שמירת הלשון שלפי שיטת הרמב"ן זה
מצוה תמידית זכירת מעשה מרים ודבר גדול עשה בתירגומו
ובביאוריו כי זה יקל לרבים ללמוד הלכות אלו וע"י הלימוד יזהרו
שלא יבואו לידי איסור.

זה מקרוב נתודע לי, ע"י מוסדות הקירוב, שע"י מצוה זו של
שמירות איסורי דיבור נתקרבו כמה מאחינו בני ישראל הנדחים
וע"י ספר זה יהי' הזדמנות יותר לקרב רחוקים.

יתברך כב' שעל ידו ירוו בני ישראל ממים חיים ויזכה להמנות בין
מזכי הרבים שצדקתם עומדת לעד.

בברכת כתוח"ט

שמואל קמנצקי

A letter from my esteemed mechutan, שליט״א

בס״ד

Rabbi Zev Leff
Rav of Moshav Matisyahu
Rosh Hayeshiva
Yeshiva Gedola Matisyahu

Teves 16, 5758

Dear Friends,

I would like to publicly extol Rabbi Dovid Marchant, שליט״א, for the important contribution he has made to the Torah world, in translating the text of the monumental work *Chofetz Chaim* by Rabbi Yisroel Meir HaCohen Kagan zt"l into English. The translation includes also the *Mekor HaChaim* and *Be'er Mayim Chayim* and a commentary called "Yad Dovid" by Rabbi Marchant.

The translation is clear, concise and professional making it a valuable aid disseminating the works of the saintly *Chofetz Chaim* amongst the English speaking community. It will serve to increase the awareness to the need of guarding one's tongue from engaging in speech contrary to Torah law.

This work is also valuable to *bnei* Torah, those who can learn the *Chofetz Chaim* from the original text. For since it emanates from an established Torah scholar it is not a mere literal translation, but serves as a guide and commentary to enlighten the reader to properly understand the text.

Rabbi Marchant has greatly benefited the Jewish community with this work and in this merit may Hashem bless him and his family – spiritually, physically and materially – to be able to toil in Torah and service to Hashem for many long, healthy years. May he merit to continue to strengthen and enhance Torah amongst the Jewish people.

With admiration and respect and Torah blessings,

Zev Leff, (Moshav Matisyahu)

CONTENTS

PREFACE

רבות מחשבות בלב איש, ועצת ה' היא תקום (משלי יט:כא)

"Many thoughts are in man's heart, but only the
counsel of Hashem will prevail" (*Mishlei* 19:21)

People make all sorts of plans for all sorts of good and righteous undertakings. As much as it is Hashem's desire that we make
these plans and try to see them through to fruition, not even the
slightest or simplest project can have any success at all unless
Hashem wills it.

Countless times it was clear that without the help of Heaven,
the best laid plans for writing and publishing this book would have
come to naught. "Give thanks to Hashem, for He is good, for His
kindness is eternal!" I thank my Creator for bestowing upon me the
understanding and strength to produce this work.

Although in manuscript I have translated and elucidated *Sefer
Chofetz Chaim, Hilchos Loshon Hora,* in its entirety, it was decided to publish this work in several stages in order to make it
available to the public sooner. This first volume includes not only
the Foreword and Chapter One of *Hilchos Loshon Hora,* but also
an extensive Overview detailing many of the principles and back-
ground concepts needed in studying this intricate subject[*]. It is
hoped that with this information in hand the reader will be able to
approach the whole topic with a feeling of familiarity. Moreover,
Chapter One itself deals with many basic concepts in the subject of
loshon hora . Thus this material was considered sufficient to com-

---

[*] In the original work the Foreword is followed by an Introduction to the
negative and positive precepts appertaining to *loshon hora* and *rechilus,*
this is in itself a whole volume and therefore it was felt best to leave it as a
separate volume in the English work.

prise the first volume and to begin presenting this work. Subsequent volumes are planned to contain several chapters each, and it is hoped that בע״ה, before long the entire work will be available to the public.

The original *Sefer Chofetz Chaim* consists of two parts: the main text, *Mekor HaChaim*, which presents the basic *halachos*; and *Be'er Mayim Chaim*, the *Chofetz Chaim's* commentary to *Mekor HaChaim*, in which he explains the sources from which he derived these *halachos*. With the help of Heaven, I was able to translate both these parts, and also to elucidate them with my own commentary, *Yad Dovid*. Wherever I added my own words in the translation itself, they are enclosed in square brackets.

For the reader's convenience, in the first part of the book each clause of *Mekor HaChaim* is followed by a brief precis (shortened version) of the relevant clauses of *Be'er Mayim Chaim,* while the full version of *Be'er Mayim Chaim* is found in the second part of the book. In the translation I have tried to stay as close as possible to the wording and arrangement of the original Hebrew (which in this edition is printed on the facing page), while presenting a smooth, readable English text. Sometimes this has required some minor rearrangement of the order, but I have not omitted any of the original work.

Hashem has granted me the merit to have given *shiurim* (classes) on *Sefer Chofetz Chaim* to many different groups of adults and youngsters in England, and to have given a daily *shiur* on this subject in *kollel* here in *Eretz Yisroel*. And now I have been granted the merit to begin publishing the unabridged, annotated English edition of *Sefer Chofetz Chaim*. Without the help of Heaven, I could not have taught or written one word.

Anyone who has studied *Sefer Chofetz Chaim* will be fully aware that there is really no end to the amount of research and dialectics which one can devote to understanding this holy work. One need only see how much scholarly debate has appeared in recent years in Hebrew commentaries on it. (Many of these commentaries are cited in this English edition; a list of them appears at the end of this sefer.) They probe the exact intent of *Chofetz Chaim* on various points, suggest answers to apparent contradictions, and so on.

To cite only two examples of disputed issues:

▪Concerning whether one is permitted to speak *loshon hora* about oneself: A Midrash cited in *Hilchos Loshon Hora* (ch. 1, *Be'er Mayim Chaim*, clause 15) states that when the Prophet Yeshayahu complained about himself and the Jewish nation: "Woe is me, for I am destroyed, for I am a man of contaminated lips, and I dwell among a people of contaminated lips!" (*Yeshayahu*, 6:5), Hashem reprimanded him: "You are allowed to say this about yourself, but you are not allowed to say it about them," the Jewish nation. *Ali Be'er* (to *Be'er Mayim Chaim* there) explains why this passage cannot serve as proof that it is permissible to speak *loshon hora* about oneself (see below, p.168, Yad Dovid "b"). However, *Ohev Yamim* (ch. 5, clause 7, and footnote there) cites this very passage as a proof that it is permissible! Both of these commentators mention (with differing interpretations, of course) the well-known story about the *Chofetz Chaim* in which he is said to have remarked that even about oneself one is forbidden to speak *loshon hora*.

▪In one issue of the journal *Marpeh Loshon* (pamphlet 3) two scholars elucidate various points throughout *Sefer Chofetz Chaim*, yet in the very next issue another scholar disputes many of these elucidations one by one!

Chofetz Chaim apparently published this holy work in the year 5633 (1873) — based on the date of one of the original approbations — and he left this world sixty years later, in 5693(1933). Such Torah giants as R' Yisroel Salanter and the Gerrer Rebbe kept a copy of the book on their tables and constantly referred to it. It is known that R' Yisroel Salanter disagreed with *Chofetz Chaim* on only one point in the book; also the author during the last sixty years of his life never revised the new editions to answer any apparent contradictions. Clearly, our generation really needs the *Chofetz Chaim* himself to explain to us many underlying meanings so that we could understand his work completely.

If so, who can really claim that he has fully mastered this holy *sefer?* Therefore, although I have done my utmost to present what *Chofetz Chaim* is saying, nevertheless, it is only fair to say that sometimes it may well be that I may fall short of perfection in the explication of his intent.

Sometimes it will be noticed that I cite a particular *halachah* in the name of some commentary, even though it seems to be stated explicitly by *Sefer Chofetz Chaim* itself. This is usually because in that particular passage the intent of *Chofetz Chaim* is open to interpretation and I wish to show that there are those who understand it in the manner cited.

It is impossible to describe in short words the amount of time and work that have gone into translating this great classic and trying to elucidate it in the clearest way possible — speaking many hours with those scholars who are involved with this subject, and sometimes spending days, weeks, and even months searching for the correct meaning of a few words in *Be'er Mayim Chaim.*

When teaching about the mitzvah of guarding our speech I always mention in the opening *shiur* an important story which substantiates the tremendous personal reward one receives for thoroughly knowing and observing the laws of *loshon hora* and *rechilus* . The story is retold by R' Shalom Schwadron, *zt"l, Maggid* of Jerusalem, about one Purim when the home of the *Chofetz Chaim* was filled with people. A certain young scholar insisted that the *Chofetz Chaim* promise him that he could sit next to him in the world to come. The *Chofetz Chaim* replied: "I don't know how big a share I have in Gan Eden, but one thing I do know — I will probably have some share in Gan Eden, because from the day I was old enough to reason and understand, I have not listened to nor spoken *loshon hora.* If you promise me that from now on you will do the same, I can assure you a place next to me in Gan

Eden."

Let us stop and think about this reply. Even if we have not personally been promised by the *Chofetz Chaim* that we may sit next to him in Gan Eden, we see that he made a clear assumption that probably, for keeping away from listening to or speaking *loshon hora,* he had some share in Gan Eden. In other words, a share in Gan Eden is assured to any Jew who observes the laws of *loshon hora.* What a tremendous revelation this is for us! Any thoughtful Jew, upon learning of this, should immediately repent of having previously listened to or spoken *loshon hora,* thus wiping his or her slate clean of this sin and embarking upon a new life of learning and observing these *halachos.*

However, even if one has made a thorough study of *Sefer Chofetz Chaim,* nevertheless without constant review one begins to forget the finer points of the laws and thus will no doubt in some way transgress the prohibition of *loshon hora.*

On the other hand, if one feels that observing all these laws in their intricate details is currently beyond his power, he still achieves greatly by observing whatever he can, as *Chofetz Chaim* writes in the preface to his work *Shemiras HaLashon* (dealing with the philosophical and aggadic aspects of guarding our speech): "One's evil inclination might persuade him to think that since he feels he cannot observe the laws of *loshon hora* in detail, it is better to keep from observing them at all. One should rebut this thought as follows: Would I follow the same reasoning to exempt myself from making a livelihood? For example, let us imagine that someone saw me running eagerly to make a certain business deal, and he asked me: 'Why bother running to such a deal? Do you think you will become the richest man in the world, like so-and-so?' I would reply to him: 'Just because I will not become as rich as so-and-so, does that mean that I should refrain from making a living?' Now, if this is so concerning a matter of the mortal body, what will I answer about that which concerns my soul? Just because I am unable to observe the law in all its intricate details, through which I would achieve an eternal level of great holiness — just because of this should I completely withdraw from supervising my soul and not guard my speech as much as I can? This is what King Shlomo, may peace be upon him, referred to when he said: 'Everything your hand finds to do, do it with your strength' (*Koheles* 9:10). It is to teach us that even if a person thinks he cannot fulfill a mitzvah in all its details, nevertheless he should do what he can."

Learning the *halachos* is essential, but beyond that, we have to make them an integral part of our daily living. It is told of R' Naftali Amsterdam (1832-1916), a close disciple of R. Yisroel Salanter, that in the midst of studying *Ketzos HaChoshen* with a learning partner he would regularly go to the door leading to his family's quarters and ask: "Is, God forbid, any *loshon hora* being spoken?" (*Hame'oros HaGedolim*).

None can deny that we are suffering the birth pangs prior to the coming of *Moshiach Tzidkenu*, and as *Chofetz Chaim* writes in his Foreword, one of the sure ways to hasten the coming of *Moshiach* is to rectify the primary reason for our long, long, bitter exile — namely, the sin of causeless hatred and *loshon hora*. In recent years we have witnessed, *Boruch Hashem*, a tremendous movement to study the laws of *loshon hora* and *rechilus*, resulting in new books, lectures, tapes, telephone learning partners, and even special evening *kollelim*. It is also amazing how many of our non-religious brothers have somehow heard about the prohibition against speaking *loshon hora*! This is a leap forward in the right direction for our nation as a whole. May we soon merit to see the end of our exile.

I hope that, among others, I will add some small contribution to this movement by making this key work, *Sefer Chofetz Chaim* available to the English-speaking public.

I now take the opportunity of thanking those who have assisted in the production of this work.

I am grateful for the encouragement of all the Gedolim *shlita*, who approved the idea of this project, and took time from their busy schedule to look over the material and write their letters of approbation.

Many busy colleagues kindly gave of their time in *pilpul chaverim*, discussing with me major and minor sections of *Sefer Chofetz Chaim*, elucidating difficult points, etc. These include R' Yitzchak Berkowitz, *shlita*, author of *A Lesson a Day*, based on *Sefer Chofetz Chaim,* R' Beryl Eisenblatt, *shlita*, the author of *Loshon Chaim* on *Sefer Chofetz Chaim*; and R' Yisroel Eisenblatt, *shlita*, a member of the Mirrer Yeshivah in Jerusalem.

I also thank all those who attended my *shiurim* on this subject; the questions they raised enabled me to reach better clarity on many points.

I wish to thank the well-known promulgator of *Chofetz Chaim's* teachings, Mr. Michael Rothchild, of the Chofetz Chaim Heritage Foundation, New York, for his assistance. May Hashem help him in all his endeavors to enlighten *Klal Yisroel* on the subject of *shmiras haloshon.*

I am grateful to Mr. Yaakov Feldheim for his encouragement and his invaluable comments and advice, through which this volume has been greatly enhanced.

Harvey Klineman made an indispensable contribution through his skill in book design.

I deeply appreciate the painstaking, patient and skillful work of Mrs. R. Reichert in typesetting this volume.

My wife Chana, תחי' has made it possible for me to sit uninterruptedly within the tent of learning, and has encouraged me constantly in this project. Words are inadequate to express my appreciation to her. May Hashem reward her and give us both health, strength and *nachas* to bring up and educate all our children שיחי' in Torah, *yiras Shomayim*, and *midos tovos.*

Last but not least, I wish to thank R' Shlomo Fox-Ashrei, *shlita*, the editor of this work, without whom the project would not have seen the light of day. He has been a constant source of help, not only through his editing expertise, but also through some of his own elucidations on *Sefer Chofetz Chaim* which are incorporated in this work.

May Hashem bless all those mentioned above, among all of *Klal Yisroel*, with success in their endeavors both spiritually and materially, to raise their families in the way of Torah.

I ask my honored readers to be so good as to inform me of any mistake they may find in this book, so that I can rectify it in future editions. Thus they will have a share in the mitzvah of bringing merit to the public.

Dovid Marchant
Jerusalem, Chanukah 5758

OVERVIEW

OVERVIEW

For the reader's convenience, some basic principles regarding the prohibitions of *rechilus* and *loshon hora* are presented here. This is only a brief outline of certain important points, and is not intended to be an exhaustive summary of the laws. There will be occasion to refer to this Overview throughout the commentary to *Mekor HaChaim* and *Be'er Mayim Chaim*.

Dovid Marchant

1. RECHILUS

1) The Torah states: "You shall not go about as a talebearer among your people" (לֹא תֵלֵךְ רָכִיל בְּעַמֶּיךָ).[1] The term for talebearer, רָכִיל means literally "peddler." Like a peddler who travels around, buying goods where they are plentiful and selling where they are scarce, the talebearer travels around, seeking out gossip in one place in order to relate it somewhere else where it is not yet known.[2]

2) The talebearing (*rechilus*) mentioned in this verse is understood by our Sages to be a report that causes hatred. The sin of *rechilus* involves three people: the talebearer, the listener, and the person spoken about; for example, Reuven (the talebearer) says something to Shimon which causes Shimon to hate Levi.[3] Thus a report can be *rechilus* even if it is not disparaging, as long as it causes the listener to hate the person

---

[1] *Vayikra* 19:16.

[2] *Sifra* and *Ramban* to our verse; the halachic significance of this analogy will be discussed below, para. 23.

[3] *Hilchos Rechilus*, ch. 1, clauses 1-3.

spoken about.[4] If it is also disparaging, the speaker has transgressed two prohibitions: *rechilus* and *loshon hora* (see below, sec. 3). For example, if someone tells Reuven: 'Shimon stole...' this is *loshon hora*. If he adds: '...your pen' it is also *rechilus*.

3) Even if the tale does not cause hatred, but merely causes the listener to be upset with the person spoken about, it is considered *rechilus*. For example, someone told a mother that her child said or did something against her. The mother will not hate her child for this, but she might get upset with the child. The one who told her has still violated the prohibition against *rechilus*.[5]

4) A report that causes hatred constitutes *rechilus* even if it is true.[6] If it contains any falsehood, the speaker has committed the even more severe transgression of *motzi shem ra*[7] (see below, para. 56).

5) Whether the "tale" is conveyed verbally or by some other means such as writing or gesture, it is included in this prohibition.[8]

6) Subject to certain conditions, it is permissible to speak *rechilus* if it is for a constructive purpose (see below, sec. 9).

---

[4] Ibid., clause 2; for an example of such a tale see *Yad Dovid* to *Hilchos Loshon Hora*, p. 155, "a".

[5] *Hilchos Rechilus*, ch. 7, clause 1.

[6] Ibid., ch. 1, clause 4.

[7] Introduction, Positive Precepts, clause 13; see also *Sefer Hilchos Loshon Hora U'Rechilus*, *Hilchos Rechilus*, ch. 2, who adds two other sources: from *Sefer Chofetz Chaim*, *Hilchos Rechilus*, ch. 7, clause 2, and *Hilchos Loshon Hora*, ch. 1, *Be'er Mayim Chaim*, clause 2.

[8] *Hilchos Rechilus*, ch. 1, clauses 9, 11.

For other cases where *rechilus* is permissible see *Hilchos Rechilus,* ch. 6, clause 9.

7) The Torah states: "You shall not carry a false report"(לֹא תִשָּׂא שֵׁמַע שָׁוְא *Shemos* 23:1). From here we derive that one may not accept a report of *rechilus*, meaning that one may not believe that the report is true.[9] (Believing the report is called *kabbalas rechilus.*) Only in certain cases is it permitted to believe *rechilus.*[10]

(Even though the term *rechilus* refers to a report that is true, nevertheless in this verse it is referred to as "false," for the reasons explained by *Chofetz Chaim* in "Negative Precepts," *Be'er Mayim Chaim,* clause 2.)

8) From the same verse we derive that it is forbidden even to listen to *rechilus*[11] even if one does not intend to believe it.[12] However, the prohibition against believing is more severe than that against listening; for if one is aware that the information can help him protect himself (or others) he may listen to it in order to take precautions in case it might be true. Nevertheless, he may not believe it. That is, even though he takes precautions, nonetheless in his mind he must accord the person the status of a completely innocent individual.[13]

The permission to listen to *rechilus* depends upon other conditions as well.[14]

---

[9] Ibid., ch. 5, clause 1.

[10] Ibid., ch. 6, clauses 3 and 9.

[11] Ibid., ch. 5, clause 2 (See *Hilchos Loshon Hora* ch.6, *Be'er Mayim Chaim,* clause 2).

[12] Ibid.

[13] Ibid.

[14] See *Hilchos Loshon Hora,* ch. 6, *Be'er Mayim Chaim,* clause 3; and see *Hilchos Rechilus,* ch. 5, *Be'er Mayim Chaim,* clause 2, which refers us to this source.

2. AVAK RECHILUS

9) *Avak* means "dust." Thus *avak rechilus* means literally, "the dust of *rechilus*." That is, it is not absolute *rechilus*, but contains a tinge of the transgression. *Chofetz Chaim* considers this to be Rabbinically forbidden.[15]

10) *Avak rechilus* is defined by *Chofetz Chaim* as a tale which would not cause the listener actually to hate or be upset with the person spoken about, but would cause him to feel irritation against him. However, *Chofetz Chaim* says that possibly even this is considered *rechilus* on the Scriptural level, since there is a very fine line between *avak rechilus* and actual *rechilus*. That is, "irritation" and "being upset" are very similar, if not identical.[16]

3. LOSHON HORA

11) *Loshon hora* means literally "evil speech." Here too three people are involved: the speaker, the listener, and the person spoken about.

12) The prohibition against *loshon hora* applies only if the disparaging information is true.[17] If it contains any falsehood the speaker has committed the even more severe transgression *motzi shem ra*[18] (see below, para. 56).

13) Sometimes the Sages use the term *loshon hora* in a general way to express that certain speech is evil, and thus the term

---

[15] See *Hilchos Loshon Hora* , ch. 1, *Be'er Mayim Chaim*, clause 8; ch. 10, *Be'er Mayim Chaim*, clause 7. (*Avak rechilus* is comparable to *avak loshon hora*; see *Hilchos Rechilus*, ch. 8, *Be'er Mayim Chaim*, clause 1.)

[16] *Hilchos Rechilus*, ch. 8, *Be'er Mayim Chaim*, clause 1. For other examples of *avak rechilus* see *Hilchos Rechilus* , ch. 8.

[17] *Hilchos Loshon Hora*, ch. 1, clause 1.

[18] Ibid.

may refer to that which is technically *rechilus*[19] or even *motzi shem ra.*[20]

14) Whether the information is conveyed verbally or by some other means such as writing or gesture, it is included in the prohibition of *loshon hora.*[21] However, the Sages used the term *loshon hora* ("evil speech") because in most cases the information is conveyed through speech.[22]

4. THE SOURCE OF THE PROHIBITION

15) *Rambam*[23] understands that the prohibition of *loshon hora* is derived *a fortiori (kal vachomer)* from the verse (quoted above) prohibiting *rechilus.* That is, if the Torah prohibits *rechilus,* which is not necessarily disparaging, then all the more so it certainly prohibits *loshon hora,*[24] which is disparaging.

16) (Perhaps we may explain *Rambam's* reasoning as follows: A human being is created by Hashem, in His image; thus to disparage someone is to disparage the handiwork of Hashem and is a direct affront to Him. *Rechilus,* although it causes hatred among people, does not constitute a direct insult to the Creator.)

---

[19] *Hilchos Loshon Hora*, ch. 2, *Be'er Mayim Chaim*, clause 3; s.v. "דרכילות" *Hilchos Rechilus* , ch. 3, *Be'er Mayim Chaim*, clause 2; גם כן לשון הרע מקרי" s.v. "ואח"כ כלל לשניהם" ; ibid., ch. 8, *Be'er Mayim Chaim*, clause 6, s.v. "וגם ידוע הוא".

[20] *Ohev Yamim*, ch. 3, clause 2. For an example, see footnote there.

[21] *Hilchos Loshon Hora*, ch. 1, clause 8.

[22] *Sefer Ohev Yamim*, ch. 3, clause 8.

[23] As explained by *Kesef Mishneh* to *Hilchos De'os* 7:1, and elaborated upon by *Chofetz Chaim* in *Hilchos Loshon Hora*, ch.1, *Be'er Mayim Chaim*, clause 4.

[24] See Hilchos Loshon Hora ch. 1 beginning of Be'er Mayim Chaim, clause 4.

17) Other early authorities, such as *Ravad* maintain that, on the contrary, *rechilus* is a more severe transgression than *loshon hora*; hence they do not derive the prohibition of *loshon hora* from our verse about *rechilus*, but from other verses.[25]

18) One category of *loshon hora* mentioned by *Chofetz Chaim* is disparagement (גְנוּת or גְנַאי).[26] This is clearly implied in a number of places throughout *Sefer Chofetz Chaim*. For example, in *Hilchos Loshon hora*, ch. 4, clause 1, he refers to *loshon hora* as relating "a matter through which the person is deprecated" (דָבָר שֶׁיִּתְבַּזֶּה עַל יְדֵי זֶה). Similarly in ch. 6, clause 10, we learn that *loshon hora* causes the value (עֵרֶךְ) of the person to be decreased in the perception of the listener. Thus the disparagement damages the good name of the person spoken about.[27] This occurs if one relates that a person has sinned against Hashem (בֵּין אָדָם לַמָּקוֹם) or against his fellow man(בֵּין אָדָם לַחֲבֵרוֹ)[28] or when one negates another's qualities (שְׁלִילַת הַמַּעֲלוֹת), i.e., his intelligence, professional ability, physical condition, or character.[29] Thus, saying that someone is stu-

---

[25] *Hilchos Loshon Hora*, ch. 1, *Be'er Mayim Chaim*, clause 4.

[26] For a second category of *loshon hora*, see below, para. 28.

[27] One might ask: Surely if one causes the listener to hate the person spoken about (*rechilus*), one also damages his good name in the eyes of the listener? If so, isn't every case of *rechilus* also *loshon hora* ? The answer is: Not always does the listener, who becomes upset with the person spoken about, also think less of him. He may see that he is right in what he said, but may nevertheless be upset over it. However, if an utterance causes the listener to be upset with the person spoken about and also to think less of him, then it is a transgression of both *rechilus* and *loshon hora*. Heard from R' Chaim Freiman, author of *Kitzur Hilchos Loshon Hora.*

[28] *Hilchos Loshon Hora*, ch. 4, clause 1.

[29] Ibid., ch. 5, clause 2.

pid, an idiot, clumsy, immature, muddle-headed, would fall under this latter category of negating someone's qualities.[30]

5. THE EFFECT OF *LOSHON HORA* (אֲהָנוּ מַעֲשָׂיו)

19) When one speaks *loshon hora* and succeeds in damaging the good name of the person spoken about, in that the listener believes the derogatory information, this is termed אֲהָנוּ מַעֲשָׂיו "his [the speaker's] deeds [of relating *loshon hora*] were effective." It is certainly a transgression of *loshon hora*. On the other hand, if the speaker does not succeed in damaging the good name of the person spoken about, because the listener does not believe the derogatory information, this is termed לֹא אֲהָנוּ מַעֲשָׂיו "his deeds were not effective." Nevertheless, it is still a transgression of *loshon hora*.[31] *Chofetz Chaim* mentions an even more extreme case of this, namely where the speaker assumes from the beginning that his report will not damage the good name of the person spoken about, because he knows the listener will not believe the derogatory information. Even in this case relating the information is a transgression of *loshon hora*.[32]

Why is this so? As clearly explained by Rabbeinu Yonah in *Shaarei Teshuvah*,[33] speaking disparagingly about someone is forbidden from two standpoints: (a) the outcome: damaging the good name of the person spoken about; (b) the intent: speaking with intent to disparage someone. Thus in the case where the speaker does not succeed or even try to dam-

---

[30] See *Hilchos Loshon Hora,* ch. 2, *Be'er Mayim Chaim,* clause 1, s.v. "ואין לומר דהתם".

[31] *Hilchos Loshon Hora,* ch. 3, *Be'er Mayim Chaim,* clause 6, based on Gemara *Erachin* 16a.

[32] *Hilchos Loshon Hora,* ch. 3, clause 6.

[33] Ch. 3, clause 216, cited by *Chofetz Chaim* in *Hilchos Loshon Hora* , ch. 3, *Be'er Mayim Chaim,* clause 7.

age the good name of the person spoken about, the disparaging utterance is still forbidden by the Torah, due to his intention to speak negatively.[34]

The practical difference between these two cases concerns the punishment of leprosy (צָרַעַת). In the case where "his deeds were effective," the speaker is punished by leprosy, while in the case where "his deeds were not effective," there is no punishment of leprosy.[35]

20) Subject to certain conditions, it is permissible to speak *loshon hora* if it is for a constructive purpose (see below, sec.9). Even if someone gives us permission to disparage him we are not permitted to do so if our intent is to reveal his disparagement (*Hilchos Loshon Hora*, ch. 2, *Be'er Mayim Chayim*, clause 28.)

21) The prohibitions against listening to and believing *rechilus* (see above, paras. 7, 8) apply to *loshon hora* as well.[36] Only in certain cases is it permitted to believe *loshon hora*.[37] The permission to listen to *loshon hora* (even without believing it) depends upon other conditions as well. [38]

6. AVAK LOSHON HORA

22) Literally, "the dust of *loshon hora*." This refers to statements which in themselves contain no disparaging or dam-

---

[34] Why does *Chofetz Chaim* mention the simpler case of לֹא אֲהָנוּ מַעֲשָׂיו when even the more extreme case is forbidden? The answer is that even though the simpler case could be deduced from the more extreme case, he wished to state both explicitly (לֹא זוּ אַף זוּ).

[35] For the implications of "leprosy" in our time, see *Reishis Chochmoh, Shaar Hakedushah,* ch. 13, who writes that it has a spiritual rather than physical manifestation.

[36] *Hilchos Loshon Hora.*, ch. 6, clauses 1 and 2.

[37] See *Hilchos Loshon Hora*, ch. 7, clauses 5 and 12.

[38] See ibid., ch. 6, *Be'er Mayim Chaim*, clause 3.

aging information and therefore are not actual *loshon hora;* however, they are such that, for example, they might lead to speaking *loshon hora.*[39] *Avak loshon hora* is Rabinically forbidden.[40]

7. INFORMATION WHICH IS PUBLIC KNOWLEDGE
(דָּבָר מְפוּרְסָט)

23) As explained above, the prohibition against *rechilus* (and, according to *Rambam, loshon hora* as well) is derived from the verse, "You shall not go about as a talebearer." The word for "talebearer" in this verse is רָכִיל, which means literally "a peddler." *Sifra*[41] explains that just as a peddler buys goods in one place and sells them in another, so too the talebearer collects information in one place and relates it in another place. *Chofetz Chaim* points out an important implication: A peddler can perform his function only if the goods he offers were previously unavailable. Similarly a person transgresses the Torah's prohibition against talebearing only if the information was unavailable to the people to whom he relates it.[42] But if the information is already known to all,

---

[39] In such a case, one might also transgress the Torah injunction: "Do not place a stumbling-block before a blind man" (*Vayikra* 19:14), which prohibits causing anyone to stumble either physically or figuratively, i.e. to commit a sin (*Hilchos Loshon Hora*, ch. 9, *Hagoh* to *Be'er Mayim Chaim*, clause 1). Other examples of *avak loshon hora* are mentioned in *Hilchos Loshon Hora*, ch. 9.

[40] Ibid., ch. 1, end of *Be'er Mayim Chaim*, clause 8; and ch. 10, *Be'er Mayim Chaim*, clause 7.

[41] To our verse.

[42] *Hilchos Loshon Hora*, ch. 2, *Be'er Mayim Chaim*, clause 4, s.v. נראה לי "דסברת"

32

then a person is permitted to repeat it to another and this is not a transgression of *loshon hora*.[43]

Thus the prohibition against *loshon hora* does not apply to information which is already public knowledge (דָּבָר מְפוּרְסָם)[44] The reason is that the information is no "news" (חִידוּשׁ) to the listener,[45] and therefore the speaker has not performed the function (פְּעוּלָה) of a talebearer, namely to make information available in a place where it was not available.

However, it appears from several places in *Sefer Chofetz Chaim*[46] that the permission to relate drogatory information which is already a matter of public knowledge applies only if one relates it incidentally (דֶּרֶךְ אַקְרַאִי), i.e., with no intent to

---

[43] Ibid. In citing *Sifra* to explain the halachic implications of the term "peddler," *Chofetz Chaim* is interpreting *Rambam*, whose subject is not a "matter of public knowledge" (דָּבָר מְפוּרְסָם) but a matter which has been revealed "in front of three people" (בְּאַפֵּי תְּלָתָא; see *Hilchos Loshon Hora*, ch. 2), and on this subject other *Rishonim* dispute *Rambam's* ruling. Nevertheless regarding a "matter of public knowledge" (דָּבָר מְפוּרְסָם), these other *Rishonim* are in agreement with *Rambam*. *Nesivos Chaim*, p. 314; *Chelkas Binyomin*, in his commentary to *Hilchos Loshon Hora*, ch. 2, *sif katan* 4.

[44] See *Hilchos Loshon Hora*, ch. 2, clause 4: אִם לֹא שֶׁכְּבָר נִתְפַּרְסֵם הַדָּבָר וְנוֹדָע לַכֹּל see also ibid., ch. 2, *Be'er Mayim Chaim*, clause 1 in the parentheses, s.v."וּאם מיירי"; ch. 3, *Be'er Mayim Chaim*, clause 12; ch. 4, *Be'er Mayim Chaim*, clauses 7 and 41; ch. 8, clause 3 in the parentheses; ch. 8, *Hagoh* to *Be'er Mayim Chaim*, clause 16; ch. 10, *Be'er Mayim Chaim*, clause 31, s.v. the second "וּלא תקשה".

[45] Ibid., ch. 5, *Be'er Mayim Chaim*, clause 8; *Hilchos Rechilus*, ch. 4, *Be'er Mayim Chaim*, clause 3. s.v. "וּמכל מקום אינו ברור לאיסור"

[46] *Hilchos Loshon Hora*, ch. 2, *Be'er Mayim Chaim*, clause 10; ch.4, *Be'er Mayim Chaim*, clause 6 s.v. "וּאין להתיר מטעם"; ch. 8, clause 3 in the parentheses; and see *Marpeh Loshon*, pamphlet 3, p. 24 and *Chelkas Binyomin*, in his commentary to *Hilchos Loshon Hora*, ch. 2, *sif katan* 10.

spread the information and make it known.[47] An example of relating derogatory information incidentally (דֶּרֶךְ אַקְרָאִי) would be the following: Reuven begins to discuss Shimon sympathetically, saying:"It is such a pity that he has debts to pay." To further emphasize this point he wishes to add: "His debts are so oppresive to him that he even came to steal." Since Reuven did not set out to spread and reveal the fact that Shimon stole, and only wants to mention it incidentally, he is permitted to do so if it is already public knowledge.

By contrast, an example of speaking with intent to spread the information would be where Reuven goes around telling people that he has a fascinating story to tell about how Shimon came to steal. *Chofetz Chaim* understands that this does not mean that the intention is to disparage Reuven,[48]

---

[47] *Kesef Mishneh* to *Hilchos De'os* 7:5. One could ask: If the information is a matter of public knowledge, how could one have any intent to spread it further afield? Surely it has already reached the ears of all? The answer is that, in the view of *Chofetz Chaim*, in such a case where it is impossible to intend to further spread the *loshon hora*, the intent to spread the *loshon hora* has a parallel: namely, intending to avail new, additional credibility to the information, i.e., to strenghten the listener's belief in it. (See *Hilchos Loshon Hora*, ch. 5, end of *Be'er Mayim Chaim*, clause 11.) This intent to avail credibility to the information puts the speaker in the category of "peddler," and thus his utterance is forbidden. This could lead one to speculate whether *Rabbeinu Yonah's* statement that the mere intent to disparage makes the utterance forbidden (see above, para. 19, "b") would apply even in the case of a matter of public knowledge (דָּבָר מְפוּרְסָם). Some conclude that *Rabbeinu Yonah* would not apply his principle to a matter of public knowledge. See *Marpeh Loshon*, pamphlet 3, pp. 60-61; *Chelkas Binyomin*, in his commentary to *Hilchos Loshon Hora*, ch. 3, in his *biurim*, *sif katan* 14.

[48] Thus this is not similar to the case discussed above (para.19) in the name of Rabbeinu Yonah, where the intent is to disparage.

rather, he merely wants to reveal "a great scoop" about Shimon.[49] Nevertheless this is forbidden.[50]

---

[49] *Ali Be'er*, p. 13, s.v. "אבל הח"ח למד".

[50] This condition that the derogatory information is permissible only if related incidentally (דרך אקראי) is mentioned by *Kesef Mishneh* in interpreting *Rambam*, whose topic is the case of information which has already been revealed "in front of three people" (באפי תלתא), i.e. the derogatory information is not yet public knowledge (דבר מפורסם) but is on its way to becoming so. Since it has already become available, the speaker is not in the category of a "peddler." In that case, says *Rambam*, one is permitted to relate the derogatory information, but only if one has no intent "to further spread and reveal" it. On this *Kesef Mishneh* comments that, rather than intending to spread and reveal the information, one must merely mention it incidentally (דרך אקראי) *Chofetz Chaim* infers that, according to *Rambam*, the very intent (כונה) to further spread and reveal the information is forbidden, just as it is when one actually does so; but (as *Kesef Mishneh* adds) if one mentions it only incidentally, this is not considered intent to reveal. (*Hilchos Loshon Hora*, ch. 2, *Be'er Mayim Chaim*, clause 3, s.v. "וטעמו פשוט".)

However, *Chofetz Chaim* points out, that *Yad Haketanah* interprets *Rambam* differently. According to *Yad Haketanah*, it is not enough that one relate it incidentally (דרך אקראי), but relating the information is permissible only if one merely mentions it peripherally (דרך אגב; see *Hilchos Loshon Hora*, ch. 2, *Hagoh* to clause 3); for example, Reuven begins to discuss the importance of having a livelihood; thus his topic of conversation does not begin with Shimon's situation; however, in the course of this topic he wishes to bring in peripherally an example: "...such as Shimon; it is a pity that he had debts to pay and therefore came to steal." In this case, he may do so; but if his main topic is Shimon, mentioning the derogatory information, even incidentally, would still be considered as speaking *loshon hora* and as spreading the information more rapidly than it would normally have spread. (See *Hilchos Loshon Hora*, ch. 2, *Be'er Mayim Chaim*, clause 7.) It appears from *Hilchos Loshon Hora*, ch. 2,

There are other conditions and limitations on the permission to relate a matter of public knowledge (דבר מפורסם) as mentioned in the following paragraphs (24-27).

24) Moreover, if the person we wish to speak about has bettered his ways, then even though the *loshon hora* is public knowledge, we are forbidden to relate it.[51] (This is clearly because after his repentance his offence is wiped out; therefore if one discusses the offence it is as if one is creating a new disparagement about him.) *Thus one must always bear in mind the likelihood that the indivudual we wish to speak about has repented and bettered his ways.*

25) When relating a matter of public knowledge the speaker may assume that the listener already knows the information. Obviously, however, if the listener is the type who does not hear the "talk of the town," then even a matter of public knowledge would be "news" to him, and one is forbidden to relate it to him unless there is some constructive purpose for doing so.[52]

26) Likewise, if the public have already been informed of the matter but do not yet fully believe it, one is forbidden to repeat the information to anyone,[53] if his intent is to strengthen the disparaging effect of the information.[54] Similarly, *Chofetz Chaim* states that even if someone has already related *loshon hora* to a certain individual, it is nevertheless forbidden for a

---

Be'er Mayim Chaim, clause 10 that this requirement that the information be mentioned only peripherally would apply even when relating a matter of public knowledge (דבר מפורסם; see *Marpeh Loshon*, pamphlet 3, p. 24.)

[51] *Hilchos Loshon Hora*, ch. 2, clause 9.

[52] But see *Nesivos Chaim*, p. 314, who understands that even if the speaker knows that the listener has not yet heard the information, it is permissible to tell him.

[53] *Hilchos Loshon Hora*, ch. 5, clause 8.

[54] *Hilchos Loshon Hora* , ch. 5, end of *Be'er Mayim Chaim*, clause 11.

second person to relate the same *loshon hora* to the same individual, if the intent of the second person is to strengthen the disparaging effect of the information.[55]

27) The permission regarding a matter of public knowledge applies only to *loshon hora*, but not to *rechilus*, since sometimes, by reminding the listener of a known matter, one could cause his hatred to increase.[56]

8. A PROBABLE CAUSE OF DAMAGE

28) Until now we have discussed statements which are forbidden because they are disparaging, or the speaker's intent is to disparage. But there is another kind of *loshon hora*. *Rambam* states that even if an utterance contains no disparagement, it is nevertheless considered *loshon hora* if it will eventually cause someone financial or bodily damage, or will distress or alarm him.[57] *Chofetz Chaim* explains that this is a form of גְּרָמָא בִּנְזִיקִין an "indirect cause of damage,"[58] meaning that one's actions have a reasonable probability of damaging someone, even though one does not directly perform the damage.

29) The explanation is as follows: In the eighth chapter of *Bava Kamma* the Gemara explains that if one directly damages a fellow Jew, one is obligated to compensate him financially. However, the Gemara states that if one causes dam-

---

[55] Ibid.

[56] *Hilchos Rechilus*, ch. 4, clause 2 and *Be'er Mayim Chaim* there, clause 3; see *Ohev Yamim*, ch. 5, clause 19; ch. 7, clause 3; *Nesivos Chaim*, p. 353, clause א.

[57] *Hilchos De'os* 7:5, cited by *Chofetz Chaim, Hilchos Loshon Hora,* ch. 5, clause 2 and in a number of other places.

[58] *Hilchos Rechilus*, ch. 9, preface to *Be'er Mayim Chaim* there.

age indirectly (גרמא בנזיקין) he is exempt from payment.[59] Nevertheless, we are forbidden to cause damage even indirectly.[60]

30) *Rambam*[61] applies this concept of indirect damage to the laws of *loshon hora*. He states that if one's utterance is an "indirect cause of damage," then the fact that it contains this element makes the utterance *loshon hora*.[62]

31) *Chofetz Chaim* interprets *Rambam* to mean that if a statement has a reasonable probability of causing damage this already makes it *loshon hora*, even if the damage has not yet occurred.[63]

32) *Rambam* would agree with *Rabbeinu Yonah* that saying something which damages someone's good name is *loshon hora* . However, *Rambam* considers this as only one form of damage and adds other cases. For example, consider the case of one who says: "Ploni is weak." This is not considered disparagement, since this defect is not Ploni's fault and he commits no wrong by being weak (although people are sometimes inclined to speak about such defects with dispar-

---

[59] *Bava Kamma* 60a.

[60] *Bava Basra* 22b.

[61] *Hilchos De'os* 7:5. For *Rambam's* source for this innovation, see *Kesef Mishneh* there, *halachah 4.*

[62] If the listener were sure to believe it, it would be direct damage. However, since the speaker does not know for certain that the listener will believe him, it is only indirect damage.

[63] The wording used by *Chofetz Chaim* in several places is: יוכל לגרום. See *Hilchos Loshon Hora*, ch. 5, clauses 2, 6; ch. 2, *Be'er Mayim Chaim*, clause 14. The concept of גרמא בנזיקין applies only to *loshon hora*, not to *rechilus (Shemiras Haloshon, Parashas Kedoshim.)* For the reason why this is so, see *Avodas Hamelech* to *Mishneh Torah, Hilchos De'os* 7:2, s.v. "ומש״ר", and *Chelkas Binyomin* in his commentary to *Hilchos Loshon Hora*, ch. 5, *sif katan 6.*

aging intent[64]). However, the statement has a reasonable probability of causing Ploni financial damage by preventing him from finding employment, and hence it is *loshon hora*. [65]

33) Thus there are two separate types of damage that can be involved with transmitting *loshon hora* (a) damage to the good name of the person spoken about; (b) damage to his body or property. If someone gives us permission to relate *loshon hora* that might damage his good name it is nevertheless forbidden to do so if our intent is to reveal his disparagement. However, if someone gives us permission to relate *loshon hora* that could damage his body or property we are permitted to do so. (*Hilchos Loshon Hora*, ch. 2, *Be'er Mayim Chaim* clause 28).

9. CONSTRUCTIVE PURPOSE

34) What is the law if one person speaks *loshon hora* or *rechilus* about another, but for a constructive purpose (*to'eles*), and without intent to disparage or cause hatred? The answer is that this is permitted (in the presence of the other conditions listed in *Hilchos Loshon hora*, ch. 10). Three main kinds of constructive purpose are: (a) to prevent harm to someone; (b) to help someone gain compensation for harm already done; (c) to prevent others from transgression by being "zealous for the truth." These three categories are explained in the following paragraphs.

---

[64] See *Hilchos Loshon Hora*, ch. 5, clause 2 — "It is forbidden to *disparage* ones fellow Jew concerning any defects in pefection of his qualities, whether in wisdom or in physical strength etc."

[65] Ibid., clause 5.

10. TO PREVENT HARM

35) Consider the following example: Reuven is about to go into business partnership with Shimon, and Levi knows that Shimon is dishonest. Levi tells Reuven — not in order to disparage Shimon, but simply to save Reuven from financial loss. In this case, Levi has not transgressed the prohibition against *loshon hora*.

36) Now, we have seen above (paras. 28-31) that even where there is no intent to disparage, nevertheless if a statement has a reasonable probability of causing damage it is considered *loshon hora* and is forbidden. Surely the statement: "Shimon is dishonest" — even without any intent to disparage — has a reasonable probability of causing damage to Shimon; for example, if he hears of it he might suffer emotional distress. Why, then, should the statement be permitted? The answer is as follows:

37) As mentioned above, the prohibition against *rechilus* (and, according to *Rambam*, against *loshon hora* as well) is found in the verse: "You shall not go about as a talebearer among your people." Now, the end of this same verse warns: "You shall not stand by the blood of your fellow Jew" (לֹא תַעֲמֹד עַל דַם רֵעֶךָ) which means that if you are aware that your fellow Jew is in danger you are obligated to try to save him. *Or HaChaim*[66] explains that the second part of the verse adds a qualification to the prohibition against talebearing: namely, that if an utterance is necessary in order to save one's fellow Jew, it is permitted and is not considered "talebearing." Thus for example, if one sees that Reuven intends to murder Shimon, one is permitted (and indeed obligated) to warn Shimon in order to save his life —even though this may cause Shimon to hate Reuven.

---

[66] To this verse.

38) *Chofetz Chaim*[67] states that this second part of the verse likewise teaches that one is permitted to speak *loshon hora* in order to save someone from entering into partnership with an unscrupulous person. (This includes not only business partnership, but any form of involvement with another, such as marriage, employment, medical treatment, etc.) In such a case one may even initiate the *loshon hora* even though it was not requested. This is the source of the permission to speak *loshon hora* for such a constructive purpose.[68] (This permission applies only in the presence of certain additional conditions. See *Hilchos Rechilus*, ch. 9, clause 2).

39) Similarly, it is permissible (if all the necessary conditions are fulfilled) to warn one's children or students not to associate with people who have certain bad character traits.[69]

40) Likewise, if one is considering employing someone, or entering into partnership or marriage, one is permitted to request information about the person's character and circumstances, even if one has hitherto heard nothing derogatory about him and one's inquiries may result in hearing derogatory information about him.[70]

11. TO HELP SOMEONE GAIN COMPENSATION

41) Another type of constructive purpose involves harm that has already occurred. The purpose of relating the derogatory

---

[67] *Hilchos Rechilus*, ch. 9, *Be'er Mayim Chaim*, clause 1, in name of the *Mechilta*.

[68] *Chofetz Chaim* mentions this permission in *Hilchos Rechilus* (there.). However, it is clear from his preface there that this also refers to the "indirect damage" (גְּרָמָא בְּנִזְיקִין) aspect of *loshon hora*.

[69] *Hilchos Loshon Hora*, ch. 4, clause 10, and *Be'er Mayim Chaim* there, clause 41.

[70] *Hilchos Loshon Hora*, ch. 4, clause 11; and see *Be'er Mayim Chaim* there, clause 44, where *Chofetz Chaim* brings three proofs for this law.

information is to help the injured party recover his loss. For example, Reuven stole from Shimon, or damaged his body or property, or embarrased him, or spoke to him in a manner causing him distress. Levi, who witnessed the event, knows that Reuven has not returned the theft, payed for the damage, or conciliated Shimon for the distressing words. In such a case, subject to certain additional conditions enumerated by *Chofetz Chaim*, Levi may speak to people about the transgressor for the constructive purpose of helping the injured party retrieve his loss.[71]

42) In telling others about Reuven's deed, Levi is conveying information that may be disparaging or damaging to Reuven. In other words, were it not for a constructive purpose, it would be *loshon hora*. In some cases it would also be *rechilus*; for example, if Shimon was unaware that Reuven had stolen from him, Levi's report may cause the victim to hate Reuven. Nevertheless, since the purpose is to help the injured party retrieve his loss, it is permissible to relate the information.[72]

43) What is the source of this permission? It cannot be derived from the verse quoted above: "You shall not stand by the blood of your fellow Jew," for that verse applies only when one can save someone from harm; but in our case the harm has already occurred.[73]

44) Instead, according to *Rabbeinu Yonah*, this permission is based on the verse: "A single witness shall not testify against a man regarding any sin...a matter shall be established by

---

[71] *Hilchos Loshon Hora* , ch. 10.

[72] Ibid., clause 1.

[73] *Ali Be'er*, p. 170.

the word of two witnesses" (עַל פִּי...עַל כָּל עָוֹן לְאִישׁ בָּאִישׁ אֶחָד עֵד יָקוּם לֹא); שְׁנֵי עֵדִים אוֹ עַל פִּי שְׁלֹשָׁה עֵדִים יָקוּם דָּבָר; *Devorim* 19:15).[74] This verse states that the earthly court can punish a person for sin only if at least two witnesses testify against him; and it forbids a single witness to give such testimony, since it would be *loshon hora*. (*Pesachim* 113b: The testimony of a pair of witnesses is not *loshon hora*, since it serves the constructive purpose of enabling the court to convict the transgressor; but since the testimony of a single witness cannot lead to conviction, it serves no constructive purpose.)

45) However, as *Rashi* (to our verse) explains, although a single witness is not allowed to testify about "any sin," he is allowed to testify regarding financial claims, the reason being that here, unlike with other sins, his testimony serves a constructive purpose — namely, to help the claimant retrieve his loss; for, on the testimony of a single witness the court can require the claimee to take an oath that he does not owe the money; and there is a possibility that, if he really is liable, he may admit the debt rather than swear falsely.

46) In short, when one person has stolen from or damaged another, the Torah allows even a single witness to report it in court for the constructive purpose of helping the claimant retrieve his loss. Rabbeinu Yonah understands from this that if the witness for some reason cannot help the injured party by testifying in court, then he is permitted to help him by relating the matter to people outside of court.[75]

---

[74] *Shaarei Teshuvah* 221, cited by *Chofetz Chaim, Hilchos Loshon Hora*, ch. 10, *Be'er Mayim Chaim*, clause 1; see also ibid., clauses 2, 5, 9, 16, 18, and elsewhere, where *Chofetz Chaim* refers to this principle as דּוּמְיָא דְּעֵד אֶחָד, "similar to [the law of] a single witness."

[75] The Torah is allowing *loshon hora* in court in order to help the claimant retrieve his loss. The court is therefore required, merely, so that an oath can be imposed to reach this goal. If this goal then can be achieved even

(It should be noted, however, that this permission applies only where one person has actively done some wrong to another. If he did not actively harm him, but simply refrained from doing him a favor, there is no permission to relate the matter to others. For example, Reuven needed a loan, and although Shimon had funds available he refused to lend. Levi witnessed this refusal. Even though Shimon transgressed the positive commandment to lend money to one's fellow Jew, Levi is not permitted to publicize the matter, since Shimon did not steal or damage Reuven's property.)[76]

47) The permission to testify in court applies even if the injured party had not known who did the damage, and on learning the truth he will feel animosity towards him. That is, the permission overrides not only the prohibition of *loshon hora*, but also that of *rechilus*. If so, the permission to relate the matter outside of court likewise overrides the prohibition of *rechilus*.[77]

12. TO BE "ZEALOUS FOR THE TRUTH" (קִנְאַת הָאֱמֶת)

48) Rabbeinu Yonah[78] mentions another possible permission for a single witness to relate *loshon hora*. He states: "A single

---

outside court it does not contradict what the Torah allows. This is clear from *Pesachim* 113b: If one singularly witnesses someone's transgression against Heaven, although he may not report it in court, nevertheless he may report it outside court to his rebbe. This being so, then in our case here where one may report it even in court, certainly he may report it outside of court.

[76] *Hilchos Loshon Hora*, ch. 5, *Be'er Mayim Chaim*, clause 4. The reason is that Reuven cannot force Shimon in court to lend to him, even if he has witnesses to testify about the refusal; therefore the analogy to the case of a single witness does not apply here.

[77] *Hilchos Loshon Hora*, ch. 10, *Be'er Mayim Chaim*, clause 2.

[78] *Shaarei Teshuvah* 221.

witness should relate what he has seen in order to be zealous for the truth."[79] Thus, as *Chofetz Chaim* explains,[80] even if there is no likelihood that relating the information will help the injured party gain compensation, nevertheless the witness is permitted to relate it to people in order to be zealous for the truth, i.e. in order to publicize the truth that so-and-so damaged so-and-so. However, Rabbeinu Yonah explains elsewhere[81] that merely desiring to publicize the truth is not by itself a sufficient constructive purpose. There must also be a possibility of accomplishing some gain, namely, the speaker must intend that when people hear what he reveals about the transgressor they will keep away from the path of evil, since they now see how people disparage sinners; and also, perhaps the sinner himself will be brought to repentance when he sees how people disparage his act.

49) *Rabbeinu Yonah* states[82] that this permission is derived from the verse: "Those who forsake Torah praise the wicked, but those who observe the Torah contend with them" (עֹזְבֵי תוֹרָה יְהַלְלוּ רָשָׁע וְשֹׁמְרֵי תוֹרָה יִתְגָּרוּ בָם *Mishlei* 28:4). This verse implies that Torah-observant people must contend with the wicked in order to distance others from their path.[83]

---

[79] It is clear in *Hilchos Loshon Hora*, ch. 10, clause 4, and *Be'er Mayim Chaim* there, that *Chofetz Chaim* understands the letter "ו" in the text of Rabbeinu Yonah to mean "or," not "and." (See also *Zeh Hashaar* to *Rabbeinu Yonah* there.)

[80] *Hilchos Loshon Hora*, ch. 10, clause 4.

[81] Aliyos HaRabbeinu Yonah, cited in Shitah Mekubetzes to Bava Basra 39a.

[82] Ibid.

[83] A different derivation for this permission is given by *Rabbeinu Yonah* in *Shaarei Teshuvah* 219; for discussion of this matter see *Ali Be'er*, pp. 179-180.

45

50) Since the permission of "to be zealous for the truth" is not derived from the law of the single witness (see above, sec.11), it overrides only the prohibition of *loshon hora*, but not *rechilus*. Thus this permission applies only where the injured party already knows who injured him.[84]

51) This permission of "to be zealous for the truth" also applies where the sinner transgressed an obligation towards Heaven (בֵּין אָדָם לַמָּקוֹם)[85] — but only if he has committed the sin several times, so it is clear that he has not repented and is thus established as being wicked.[86] If he has transgressed only once or twice, it could well be that in his heart he has repented.[87] If so, there is no permission to be zealous for the truth, since it is not true that he is wicked. On the other hand, in the case of theft, damage, or the like (בֵּין אָדָם לַחֲבֵרוֹ) even if it is the first offense, one is permitted to publicize it in order to be zealous for the truth; because as long as the perpetrator has not paid for the damage, it is clear that he has not regretted his act.

13. OTHER CONSTRUCTIVE PURPOSES

52) Other purposes that are considered constructive are mentioned in various places throughout *Sefer Chofetz Chaim*.

53) Conveying information merely because it is interesting or exciting is not considered a constructive purpose. Therefore, although the speaker does not specifically intend to disparage, but only to create interest or excitement, nevertheless the utterance is forbidden if it would damage the good name

---

[84] *Hilchos Loshon Hora*, ch. 10, *Be'er Mayim Chaim*, clause 18.

[85] *Hilchos Loshon Hora*, ch. 4, *Be'er Mayim Chaim*, clause 32, sub-clause 4.

[86] Ibid, ch. 4, clause 7.

[87] Ibid, clause 4.

of the person spoken about, or if it has a reasonable probability of causing him bodily or financial damage, distress, or alarm.

14. AGAINST HEAVEN—AGAINST ONE'S FELLOW MAN

54) One who speaks *loshon hora* sins against Heaven, since he violates the will of Hashem by transgressing His command: "You shall not go about as a talebearer among your people" (*Vayikra* 19:16).[88]

55) If the *loshon hora* causes bodily, financial, or emotional damage — for example, if the person spoken about hears of it and suffers emotional distress from it — then it also becomes a sin against one's fellow man.[89]

15. FALSE SLANDER (*MOTZI SHEM RA*)

56) *Motzi shem ra* means literally, "he brings forth a bad name." That is, the speaker brings forth — from his own i n vention , not from anything that actually happened — derogatory information about someone. The expression is borrowed from *Devorim* 22:14, concerning a man who falsely accuses his bride of adultery. *Sefer Mitzvos* Gadol[90] explains that the transgression of *motzi shem ra* is derived *a fortiori* (*kal*

---

[88] Ibid., ch. 4, clause 12. If the *loshon hora* was a disparaging statement, it still may not be a sin against one's fellow man, for *Chofetz Chaim* does not consider damage to someone's good name as a sin against one's fellow man [even though, as mentioned above, para. 32, it is considered an "indirect cause of damage" (גרמא בנזיקין)]. This is clear from *Hilchos Loshon Hora* ch. 4, clause 12. For further discussion of this point see *Chelkas Binyomin*, in his commentary to *Hilchos Loshon Hora* , ch. 4, *sif katan* 39.

[89] Ibid.

[90] Negative Precepts, clause 9.

vechomer) from the verse, "You shall not go about as a tale-bearer." If we derive from this verse that *rechilus* and *loshon hora* are forbidden, even though they are true statements, then certainly *motzi shem ra* is forbidden.[91] That is, since it is false it is an even more severe transgression than *rechilus* and *loshon hora*. *Rabbeinu Yonah*[92] states that *motzi shem ra* incurs the punishment of death at the hands of heaven.

This completes an outline of some basic principles regarding *rechilus* and *loshon hora*.

---

[91] See *Hilchos Loshon Hora*, ch. 1, *Be'er Mayim Chaim*, clause 3.
[92] *Shaarei Teshuvah* 3:55.

ספר

חפץ חיים

עשה'כ

מי האיש החפץ חיים וכו' נצור לשונך מרע וכו'

הוא חבור מיוסד

על הלכות איסורי לשה"ר ורכילות ואבק שלהן

ויבואר בו כל חלקי איסוריהן בכלליהן ובפרטיהן על פי הלכה היוצאת
מן התלמוד והפוסקים ראשונים ואחרונים

ממנו יוצאים שני שריגים הנושאים ספוב הארץ והאוכל פרים יחי' חיי נצח

הפנים יקרא בשם מקור החיים עשה"כ כי מוצאי מצא חיים ·
ונאמר מי האיש החפץ חיים · בו יבואר עקרי ההלכה בקיצור ·

ובאור סביב לו יקרא בשם באר מים חיים לבאר בו טעמי ההלכות והלוקיחן באריכות

וגם יגלה בו תבאר שדליתי ממנו המים חיים להראות כל דין ודין את מקור שרשו מן הש"ס והפוסקים

ונחלק לשני חלקים

א) הלכות איסורי לשה"ר . ב) הלכות איסורי רכילות .

ובשיזכני כ"י אחבר עוד חלק אחד אבר בו יקובץ כל מאמרי חז"ל מש"ס ומדרשים וזוהר סקדום כסוגכים ענינים כאלו
ומי שירלה לידע את מנין כלאוין וכעבין סכאין פ"י עון לסה"ר ורכילות יעיין כנפתח דכרנו שם כאברכנו בזה כיו כי'·

Facsimile of title page of the first edition of *Sefer Chofetz Chaim* published in 5633 (1873).

SEFER CHOFETZ CHAIM

FOREWORD

[Hashem gave us the mitzvos for our good.]

Blessed is Hashem, God of Israel, Who distinguished us from all the nations, gave us His Torah, and brought us into the Holy Land so that we could merit to fulfill all His mitzvos. His whole intention is only for our good, so that through this we should be consecrated to Him, as it is written (Bamidbar 15:40): "So that you should remember and do all My mitzvos, and you will be consecrated to your God." This enables us to receive the outpouring of His goodness and His great kindness in this world and in the world to come, as it is written (Devorim 10:12-13): "What does Hashem your God ask of you? Only to observe the mitzvos of Hashem and His statutes, for your good." (See the commentary of Ramban there, who explains that the phrase, "for your good" refers back to the beginning of the verse, "What does Hashem your God ask of you?" [a])

Not only did He give us His precious instrument [the Torah], but He also commanded us not to abandon it, as it is written: (*Mishlei* 4:2): "For I have given you good teachings; do not abandon My Torah." This is in contrast to the typical trait of human beings; for if one person gives another a fine gift, and the recipient does not treat it properly and does not consider it precious, the giver eagerly looks forward to the day when the recipient will abandon it altogether so that he [the giver] will be able to retrieve it for himself. But this is not the way our God has dealt with us; for in every generation during the time of the First Temple He gave us prophets to bring us back to the good path.

Yad Dovid

a. **ask of you:** That is, whatever He asks of you, He asks it for no other reason than for your good.

הקדמה

בָּרוּךְ ה' אֱלֹהֵי יִשְׂרָאֵל אֲשֶׁר הִבְדִּילָנוּ מִכָּל הָעַמִּים וְנָתַן לָנוּ תּוֹרָתוֹ וְהִכְנִיסָנוּ לָאָרֶץ הַקֹּדֶשׁ כְּדֵי שֶׁנִּזְכֶּה לְקַיֵּם כָּל מִצְווֹתָיו. וְכָל כַּוָּנָתוֹ הִיא רַק לְטוֹבָתֵנוּ כְּדֵי שֶׁעַל-יְדֵי זֶה נִהְיֶה קְדוֹשִׁים אֵלָיו, כְּמוֹ שֶׁכָּתוּב: לְמַעַן תִּזְכְּרוּ וַעֲשִׂיתֶם אֶת כָּל מִצְוֹתָי וִהְיִיתֶם קְדֹשִׁים לֵאלֹהֵיכֶם, וְיִהְיֶה בִּיכָלְתֵּנוּ לְקַבֵּל אֶת הַשְׁפָּעַת טוּבוֹ וְרֹב חַסְדּוֹ בָּעוֹלָם הַזֶּה וּבָעוֹלָם הַבָּא, כְּמוֹ שֶׁכָּתוּב (דברים י, יב): מָה ה' אֱלֹהֶיךָ שֹׁאֵל מֵעִמָּךְ כִּי אִם וכו' לִשְׁמֹר אֶת מִצְוֹת ה' וְאֶת חֻקֹּתָיו אֲשֶׁר אָנֹכִי מְצַוְּךָ הַיּוֹם לְטוֹב לָךְ (וְעַיֵּן שָׁם בְּפֵרוּשׁ הָרַמְבַּ"ן דְּהַאי "לְטוֹב לָךְ" אַתְּחָלַת הַפָּסוּק דְּ"מָה ה' אֱלֹהֶיךָ שֹׁאֵל מֵעִמָּךְ" קָאֵי).

וְלֹא דַּי בָּזֶה שֶׁנָּתַן לָנוּ אֶת כְּלִי חֶמְדָּתוֹ, אַף גַּם צִוָּה אוֹתָנוּ שֶׁלֹּא נַעַזְבֶנָּה, כְּמוֹ שֶׁכָּתוּב: כִּי לֶקַח טוֹב נָתַתִּי לָכֶם תּוֹרָתִי אַל תַּעֲזֹבוּ. וְלֹא כְּמִדַּת בָּשָׂר-וָדָם, שֶׁאִם יִתֵּן לַחֲבֵרוֹ מַתָּנָה טוֹבָה, וַחֲבֵרוֹ אֵינוֹ מִתְנַהֵג בָּהּ כַּשּׁוּרָה וְאֵינָהּ חֲבִיבָה בְּעֵינָיו, הוּא חוֹמֵד וּמְצַפֶּה מָתַי יַפְקִירָהּ חֲבֵרוֹ מִכֹּל וָכֹל וְהוּא יַחֲזֹר וְיִזְכֶּה בָּהּ; אֲבָל לֹא כֵן חֵלֶק אֱלֹהֵינוּ, כִּי הֵקִים לָנוּ בְּכָל דּוֹר וָדוֹר בִּימֵי בַּיִת רִאשׁוֹן נְבִיאִים לַהַחֲזִירֵנוּ לַמּוּטָב,

[When we are in our land and the Temple is standing, this gives us the opportunity to do all the mitzvos and thus to perfect every part of our soul.]

By the time of the Second Temple the spiritual state of the Jewish nation had declined, due to our many sins, and they were lacking five things[a] that had been present in the First Temple (*Yoma* 21b). Nevertheless, since we were in our land and we had the Holy Temple we could fulfill all the mitzvos of the Torah,[b] and thus we could perfect all the parts of the soul that are found within us; for in the soul [as in the body] there are 248 spiritual limbs and 365 spiritual sinews[c]. [For a detailed discussion of these parts of the soul] see *Shaarei Kedushah* by Rabbeinu Chaim Vital, section 1, gate 1.

Yad Dovid

a. **five things:** These were: (1) the Ark with its golden lid and cherubim; (2) the heavenly fire that consumed the offerings; (3) the Divine Presence (*Shechinah*); (4) prophetic inspiration (*ruach hakodesh*); and (5) the *Urim* and *Tumim*.

b. **all the mitzvos of the Torah:** This is in contrast to our situation in exile, when we cannot fulfill the mitzvos that are dependent upon the Land, nor the mitzvos connected with the Temple.

52

וְאַף בִּימֵי בַּיִת שֵׁנִי, שֶׁיָּרַד מַצַּב הַיִּשְׂרְאֵלִי בַּעֲווֹנוֹתֵינוּ הָרַבִּים מִקְּדֻשָּׁתוֹ
הָרִאשׁוֹנָה וְחָסְרוּ לָהֶם חֲמִשָּׁה הַדְּבָרִים שֶׁהָיוּ לָהֶם בְּבַיִת רִאשׁוֹן, עִם
כָּל זֶה בִּהְיוֹתֵנוּ עַל אַדְמָתֵנוּ וְהָיָה לָנוּ בֵּית הַבְּחִירָה הָיִינוּ יְכוֹלִים לְקַיֵּם
כָּל מִצְווֹת הַתּוֹרָה, וּבָזֶה הָיִינוּ יְכוֹלִים לְהַשְׁלִים כָּל חֶלְקֵי הַנֶּפֶשׁ
הַנִּמְצָאִים בָּנוּ, כִּי בַּנֶּפֶשׁ יֵשׁ גַּם-כֵּן רְמַ"ח אֵיבָרִים וּשָׁסָ"ה גִידִים
רוּחָנִיִּים (וְעַיֵּן בְּ"שַׁעֲרֵי קְדֻשָּׁה לְמוֹרֵנוּ הָרַב חַיִּים וִיטַאל, פֶּרֶק א).

Yad Dovid

c. **248 spiritual limbs and 365 spiritual sinews:** Together these total 613,
corresponding to the 613 Scriptural mitzvos. Each mitzvah which a person
fulfills, perfects one of these limbs or sinews. Thus by fulfilling all the
mitzvos he becomes perfected.

[Loshon Hora caused the Destruction and Exile.]

At the end of the period of the Second Temple period, causeless hatred and loshon hora[a] became prevalent among us, due to our many sins, and for this reason the Temple was destroyed and we were exiled from our land,[b] as is stated in Yoma (9b) and in the Jerusalem Talmud (Yoma 1:1).

(Although the Gemara there mentions only causeless hatred, the intent is also to the loshon hora which results from such hatred;[c] otherwise the punishment would not have been so severe.[d] [The *Chofetz Chaim* now brings other proofs that when the Gemara mentions causeless hatred as the reason for the Destruction, its intent is to loshon hora as well.] This is why the Gemara there concludes: "This is to teach you that causeless hatred is as destructive as idolatry, adultery, and murder"[e] and this same statement appears in Tractate *Erachin* (15b) regarding loshon hora.[f]

Yad Dovid

a. **loshon hora:** For the definition of loshon hora see Overview, sec. 3.

b. **we were exiled from our land:** Hence we could no longer observe all the mitzvos.

c. **which results from such hatred:** When people hate each other they speak *loshon hora* about each other.

d. **would not have been so severe:** Perhaps one could explain the *Chofetz Chaim's* reasoning as follows: We know that punishment is meted out "measure for measure" (see *Sotah* 8b and *Sanhedrin* 90a). Now, hatred is a personal, inner feeling which does not necessarily damage the other. *Loshon hora*, however, causes real damage to the one spoken about (for example, when it harms his good name). Hence, measure for measure, the punishment for *loshon hora* is more damaging than that for causeless hatred.

אַךְ לִבְסוֹף יְמֵי בַּיִת שֵׁנִי גָּבְרָה שִׂנְאַת חִנָּם וְלָשׁוֹן הָרָע בֵּינֵינוּ
בַּעֲוֹנוֹתֵינוּ הָרַבִּים, וּבַעֲבוּר זֶה נֶחֱרַב הַבַּיִת וְגָלִינוּ מֵאַרְצֵנוּ, כִּדְאִיתָא
בְּיוֹמָא (ט:) וּבִירוּשַׁלְמִי פֶּרֶק א' דְּיוֹמָא. (הֲגַם שֶׁהַגְּמָרָא נָקְטָה שִׂנְאַת
חִנָּם, הַכַּוָּנָה הִיא עַל לָשׁוֹן הָרָע גַּם-כֵּן שֶׁיּוֹצֵאת מִצַּד הַשִּׂנְאָה, דְּאִי לָאו
הָכֵי לֹא הָיוּ נֶעֱנָשִׁים כָּל-כָּךְ. וְהַיְנוּ דְּסַיֵּם שָׁם: לְלַמֶּדְךָ, שֶׁקָּשָׁה שִׂנְאַת
חִנָּם כְּנֶגֶד עֲבוֹדָה-זָרָה וְגִלּוּי-עֲרָיוֹת וּשְׁפִיכוּת-דָּמִים, וְזֶה מָצִינוּ
בַּעֲרָכִין (דַּף טו:) גַּבֵּי לָשׁוֹן הָרָע.

Yad Dovid

e. **idolatry, adultery and murder:** The Gemara had previously stated that
the First Temple was destroyed because of idolatry, adultery and murder,
while the Second Temple was destroyed because of causeless hatred.
Therefore it concludes that causeless hatred is as harmful as those three
sins.

f. **regarding *loshon hora*:** Only regarding *loshon hora* do we find that the
Gemara elsewhere equates its severity to these three sins. Therefore when
the Gemara here in *Yoma* equates causeless hatred to these three sins, it
must be because the hatred resulted in *loshon hora*. Thus when the Gemara
states that causeless hatred was the reason for the Destruction, it means
`causeless hatred and everything it includes,' i.e. *loshon hora*. But in fact the
punishment came particularly because of the element of *loshon hora*.

Furthermore, what we have written can be proved from that very passage itself in *Yoma;* for the Gemara there asks: "And during the time of the First Temple [did causeless hatred not prevail? But surely it is written: "Legions of those who kill by the sword shall be upon My people" (*Yechezkel* 21:17), and R' Elazar said: `This refers to people who eat and drink together and then stab each other [with the swords of their tongue!'"ᵃ] (See the Gemara there.)

Ever since that time [of the Destruction] we have been waiting and praying to the Holy One, Blessed is He, that He should draw us close [to Him by redeeming us from exile] as He promised us many times in His holy Torah and through His prophets. But our prayer is not accepted before Him, as the Sages said in Tractate *Berachos* (32b): "From the day the Temple was destroyed, an iron wall separates Israel from their Father in heaven."

In truth it is not against Him that we have to complain (heaven forbid), but only against ourselves; for from His side nothing (heaven forbid) prevents Him [from redeeming us], as it is written in *Yeshayahu* (59:1-2): "Behold, Hashem's hand is not too short to save, nor His ear too heavy to hear. Rather, your sins [have been separating you from your God, and your transgressions have hidden His face from you, that He will not hear]." And in the time of R' Yehoshua ben Levi we find (*Perek Chelek, Sanhedrin* 98a) that [when he asked Eliyahu the Prophet when *Moshiach* would come] he was told that he would come "Today, if you will listen to

Yad Dovid

a. **the swords of their tongue:** Thus it is clear that when the Gemara speaks of "causeless hatred" it refers to *loshon hora.*

וְעוֹד, מִגוּפָא דִּשְׁמַעְתָּא דְּיוֹמָא מוּכָח כְּמוֹ שֶׁכָּתַבְנוּ, מִדְּפָרִיךְ שָׁם:
וּבְמִקְדָּשׁ רִאשׁוֹן וְכוּ' וְדוֹקְרִין אֶת חַבְרֵיהֶן וְכוּ', עַיֵּן שָׁם)

וּמֵאָז וְעַד עַתָּה בְּכָל יוֹם אָנוּ מְצַפִּים וּמִתְפַּלְלִים לִפְנֵי
הַקָּדוֹשׁ-בָּרוּךְ-הוּא שֶׁיְּקָרֵב אוֹתָנוּ כַּאֲשֶׁר הִבְטִיחָנוּ בְּתוֹרָתוֹ הַקְּדוֹשָׁה
וְעַל-יְדֵי נְבִיאָיו כַּמָּה פְּעָמִים, וְאֵין מִתְקַבֶּלֶת תְּפִלָּתֵנוּ לְפָנָיו, כְּמוֹ
שֶׁאָמְרוּ חֲכָמֵינוּ זִכְרוֹנָם לִבְרָכָה בִּבְרָכוֹת (לב:) מִיּוֹם שֶׁנֶּחֱרַב
בֵּית-הַמִּקְדָּשׁ חוֹמָה שֶׁל בַּרְזֶל מַפְסֶקֶת בֵּין יִשְׂרָאֵל לַאֲבִיהֶם שֶׁבַּשָּׁמַיִם.

וּבֶאֱמֶת לֹא עָלָיו, חַס וְשָׁלוֹם, הוּא תְלוּנָתֵנוּ כִּי אִם עַל עַצְמֵנוּ, כִּי
מִצִּדּוֹ לֹא יִבָּצֵר, חַס וְשָׁלוֹם, כְּמוֹ שֶׁכָּתוּב (יְשַׁעְיָה נט, א-ב): הֵן לֹא
קָצְרָה יַד ה' מֵהוֹשִׁיעַ וְלֹא כָבְדָה אָזְנוֹ מִשְּׁמוֹעַ. כִּי אִם עֲוֹנוֹתֵיכֶם וְגוֹ'.
וּבִימֵי רַבִּי יְהוֹשֻׁעַ בֶּן לֵוִי נִמְצָא בַּגְּמָרָא סַנְהֶדְרִין בְּפֶרֶק חֵלֶק (צח.)
שֶׁהֱשִׁיבוּ לוֹ שֶׁהַיּוֹם אִם בְּקוֹלִי תִשְׁמָעוּן יָבוֹא מָשִׁיחַ, אַף שֶׁלֹּא נִשְׁלַם

[Hashem's] voice" (*Tehillim* 95:7). This was true even though
at that time the full length of exile that had been decreed
upon Israel had not yet elapsed. For it was decreed that
Israel should be in exile for one thousand years[a] which, the
Sages tell us[b] is equal to one day of the Holy One, Blessed is
He. Nevertheless [even though in the time of R' Yehoshua
ben Levi the thousand years had not yet elapsed], the power
of repentance ["if you will listen to His voice"] would have
annulled the decree. How much the more so in our time,
which is already more than eight hundred years after[c] the
end of that decreed time! Thus the reason [why *Moshiach* has
not come] is only from our side: By our many sins we are
preventing the Divine Presence from dwelling among us.

Now, when we "search our ways and examine"[d] which
sins are the main ones that have prolonged our exile, we
shall find many. But the sin of *loshon hora* is first and
foremost, for a number of reasons: For one, because this was
the main cause of our exile, as we mentioned above in the
name of Tractate *Yoma* and the Jerusalem Talmud. If so, as
long as we do not see to it that this sin is remedied, how can
the redemption come? Since this sin was so damaging that
[because of it] we were exiled from our land, then all the
more so it can prevent us from returning to our land.

Yad Dovid

a. **one thousand years**: At the time of R' Yehoshua ben Levi, Israel had
been in exile only about two hundred years. (See *Shem HaGedolim*, by the
Chida, ma'areches gedolim 1, clause 219, which states that one thousand
years is the decreed length of exile, based on *Eichah* 1:13: "He made me
desolate and ill all the day," where, as explained below, "day" means one
thousand years.)

b. **the Sages tell us**: See Sanhedrin 97a and Rashi there s.v. יחו where he
says this is derived from the verse in Tehillim (90:4): "For a thousand
years are like yesterday in Your eyes".

אָז עֲדַיִן זְמַן הַגָּלוּת שֶׁנִּגְזַר עַל יִשְׂרָאֵל שֶׁיִּהְיוּ אֶלֶף שָׁנִים בַּגָּלוּת כְּמִנְיַן
יוֹמוֹ שֶׁל הַקָּדוֹשׁ-בָּרוּךְ-הוּא, כְּמוֹ שֶׁמָּצִינוּ בְּדִבְרֵי חֲזַ"ל, עִם כָּל זֶה הָיָה
כֹּחַ הַתְּשׁוּבָה מְבַטֵּל אֶת הַגְּזֵרָה. וְכָל-שֶׁכֵּן בִּזְמַנֵּנוּ, שֶׁזֶּה יוֹתֵר מִשְׁמוֹנֶה
מֵאוֹת שָׁנָה שֶׁכָּלָה הַיּוֹם הַנַּ"ל, וְאֵין הַסִּבָּה כִּי אִם מִצִּדֵּנוּ שֶׁבַּעֲוֹונוֹתֵינוּ
הָרַבִּים אֵין אָנוּ מַנִּיחִים לוֹ שֶׁיַּשְׁרֶה שְׁכִינָתוֹ בְּתוֹכֵנוּ.

וְכַאֲשֶׁר נַחְפְּשָׂה דְּרָכֵינוּ וְנַחְקֹרָה אֵיזֶה עֲוֹונוֹת הֵם הָעִקָּרִים הַגּוֹרְמִים
לַאֲרִיכַת גָּלוּתֵנוּ, נִמְצָאֵם הַרְבֵּה, אַךְ חֵטְא הַלָּשׁוֹן הוּא עַל כֻּלּוֹ מִפְּנֵי
כַּמָּה טְעָמִים. אֶחָד, כֵּיוָן שֶׁזֶּה הָיָה הָעִקָּר לְסִבַּת גָּלוּתֵנוּ כְּמוֹ שֶׁהֱבִיאָנוּ
מִגְּמָרָא יוֹמָא וּמִירוּשַׁלְמִי הַנַּ"ל, אִם-כֵּן כָּל כַּמָּה שֶׁלֹּא נִרְאֶה לְתַקֵּן זֶה
הַחֵטְא אֵיךְ תּוּכַל לִהְיוֹת גְּאֻלָּה, כֵּיוָן שֶׁזֶּה הַחֵטְא פָּגַם כָּל-כַּךְ שֶׁעַל-יְדֵי
זֶה גָּלִינוּ מֵאַרְצֵנוּ עַל אַחַת כַּמָּה וְכַמָּה שֶׁאֵינוֹ מַנִּיחֵנוּ לָבוֹא לְאַרְצֵנוּ.

Yad Dovid

c. **eight hundred years after:** The exile was only decreed to last 1,000 years
after the Destruction. At the time when *Chofetz Chaim* wrote his work,
more than 1,800 years had already passed since the Destruction. Thus the
decreed time of exile has long since ended, and surely the power of
repentance can bring *Moshiach*.

d. **"search our ways and examine:"** Eichah 3:40.

Moreover, it is known that the exile was already decreed upon us from when the Spies committed their sin[a], as it is written in *Tehillim* (106:26-27): "He raised His hand to them [in an oath], to cast them down...among the nations and to scatter them among the lands" as this matter is explained by *Rashi* to this verse and *Ramban*[c] to *Chumash BaMidbar [14:1], Parashas Shelach.* Now, the sin of the Spies was the transgression of *loshon hora*, as is stated in *Erachin* [15a]. If so, we must remedy this sin before the redemption [can take place].

Furthermore, it is explicitly stated that this sin causes Israel to be subjected to crushing servitude, for it is written in *Parashas Shemos* (2:14) [that after Moshe slew the Egyptian and hid him in the sand, he saw Dosson and Aviram quarreling and reprimanded the wrongdoer, who replied: "Do you intend to kill me as you killed the Egyptian?" Then Moshe feared and said:] "Surely the matter is known." See

Yad Dovid

a. when the Spies committed their sin: See *BaMidbar*, chs. 13-14.

וְעוֹד, הֲלוֹא יָדוּעַ הוּא שֶׁנִּגְזַר עָלֵינוּ גָּלוּת מִכְּבָר מֵעֵת מַעֲשֵׂה הַמְרַגְּלִים, כְּמוֹ שֶׁכָּתוּב (תהלים קו): וַיִּשָּׂא יָדוֹ לָהֶם לְהַפִּיל אוֹתָם וְגוֹ' בַּגּוֹיִם וּלְזָרוֹתָם בָּאֲרָצוֹת, וּכְמוֹ שֶׁפֵּרֵשׁ רַשִׁ"י שָׁם וְהָרַמְבַּ"ן בַּחֲמֵשׁ פָּרְשַׁת שְׁלַח. וְחֵטְא הַמְרַגְּלִים הֲלוֹא הָיָה עֲוֹן לָשׁוֹן הָרָע, וּכְמוֹ דְּאִיתָא בָּעֲרָכִין (טו), אִם-כֵּן אָנוּ מֻכְרָחִין לְתַקֵּן זֶה הַחֵטְא קֹדֶם הַגְּאֻלָּה.

וְעוֹד נִמְצָא מְפֹרָשׁ שֶׁעֲוֹן זֶה גּוֹרֵם שֶׁיִּהְיוּ יִשְׂרָאֵל נִרְדִּים בְּפֶרֶךְ, מִמַּה שֶׁכָּתוּב בְּפָרְשַׁת שְׁמוֹת: אָכֵן נוֹדַע הַדָּבָר, וְעַיֵּן בְּפֵרוּשׁ רַשִׁ"י שָׁם. וְעוֹד

Yad Dovid

c. *Rashi...* and *Ramban:* They explain that it was on the ninth of Av that the people wept over the report of the Spies. Hence Hashem decreed that since they had wept needlessly that night, they would have real cause to weep on that night in future generations; for on that date both Temples would be destroyed and the Jewish People would be 'cast down among the nations.'

the commentary of *Rashi* there.[a]

In addition, it is stated explicitly in *Midrash Rabbah*, *[Devorim,] Parashas Seitzei* [6:14]: "Said the Holy One, Blessed is He: 'In this world, because there was *loshon hora* among you,[b] I removed My Presence from among you...But in the time to come [I shall take away the evil inclination from among you...and I shall return My Presence to be among you...']"

Moreover, we have an explicit verse in *Parashas Berachah* (*Devorim* 33:5): "He will be King in Yeshurun, when the heads of the people and the tribes of Israel are gathered together." *Rashi* explains there, citing *Sifri*: "When is He [Hashem, revealed as] the King of Yeshurun [the Jewish People]? Only when 'the tribes of Israel are gathered together' in unity,[c] but not when they are divided into [quarreling] groups." And it is known that this matter [of divisiveness] usually comes about through *loshon hora*.

Yad Dovid

a. **the commentary of *Rashi* there:** *Rashi* cites the *Midrash* which explains that Moshe felt distressed because he saw among Israel wicked men who spoke *loshon hora*. He thought: 'Now I understand the matter about which I have been puzzled: How have Israel sinned more than all the seventy nations, that they should be subjected to this crushing servitude? But now I see that they deserve it' [due to *loshon hora*].

b. **Our version of *Midrash Rabbah* reads:** "...because there are *baalei loshon hora* among you..." and for a discussion of the term *baalei loshon hora* see below, *Hilchos Loshon Hora*, ch. 1, .*Be'er Mayim Chaim*, clause 6.

נִמְצָא מְפֹרָשׁ בְּמִדְרַשׁ רַבָּה פָּרָשַׁת תֵּצֵא: אָמַר הַקָּדוֹשׁ-בָּרוּךְ-הוּא:
בָּעוֹלָם הַזֶּה עַל-יְדֵי שֶׁהָיָה לָשׁוֹן הָרַע בֵּינֵיכֶם סִלַּקְתִּי שְׁכִינָה מִבֵּינֵיכֶם,
אֲבָל לֶעָתִיד לָבוֹא וְכוּ'. וְעוֹד מִקְרָא מְפֹרָשׁ בְּפָרָשַׁת בְּרָכָה: וַיְהִי
בִישֻׁרוּן מֶלֶךְ בְּהִתְאַסֵּף רָאשֵׁי עָם יַחַד שִׁבְטֵי יִשְׂרָאֵל, וּפֵרֵשׁ רַשִׁ״י שָׁם
(וְהוּא מַאֲמַר הַסִּפְרִי) שֶׁאֵימָתַי הוּא מֶלֶךְ בִּישׁוּרוּן דַּוְקָא כְּשֶׁהֵם בְּיַחַד
שִׁבְטֵי יִשְׂרָאֵל וְלֹא אֲגֻדּוֹת אֲגֻדּוֹת, וְיָדוּעַ דְּדָבָר זֶה רָגִיל לָבוֹא עַל-יְדֵי
לָשׁוֹן הָרָע.

Yad Dovid

c. **in unity:** When the Jewish People are unified and at peace with each
other, Hashem allows them to live in their land and serve Him in the
Temple, and then His kingship over them is evident to all.

Besides this, how can we receive the blessings of the Holy One, Blessed is He, for which we hope, when due to our many sins we are habituated to this transgression? For after all, the Torah has put an explicit curse upon it: "Cursed is he who smites his fellow in secret" [*Devorim* 27:24], which refers to *loshon hora*, as *Rashi* explains there. This is in addition to the other curses there which apply to *loshon hora*, as explained below at the end of the Introduction.

[Loshon Hora brings severe punishment upon the transgressor.]

Besides this, we know from the Gemara mentioned above (*Erachin* 15b) that the gravity of this sin is immeasurable, so much so that the Sages say [about the transgressor] that he is like one who (heaven forbid) denies the existence of God. And the Jerusalem Talmud (*Pe'ah* 1:1) says that for this transgression a person is punished in this world, while his main punishment is reserved for the world to come.[a]

Yad Dovid

a. **the world to come:** In fact what the Gemara means is that he has no portion in the world to come, as *Chofetz Chaim* proves below, *Hilchos Loshon Hora*, ch.1, *Be'er Mayim Chaim*, clause 6.

וּלְבַד זֶה, אֵיךְ יְכוֹלוֹת לָחוּל עָלֵינוּ בִּרְכוֹתָיו שֶׁל הַקָּדוֹשׁ-בָּרוּךְ-הוּא

שֶׁאָנוּ מְקַוִּים לָזֶה כֵּיוָן דְּבַעֲווֹנוֹתֵינוּ הָרַבִּים אָנוּ מְרֻגָּלִים בְּחֵטְא זֶה,

הֲלוֹא יֵשׁ עַל זֶה אָרוּר מְפֹרָשׁ בַּתּוֹרָה: אָרוּר מַכֵּה רֵעֵהוּ בַּסָּתֶר, שֶׁהוּא

קָאֵי עַל לָשׁוֹן הָרָע כְּמוֹ שֶׁפֵּרֵשׁ רַשִׁ"י שָׁם, וּלְבַד שְׁאָר אָרוּאִין שֶׁיֵּשׁ שָׁם

עוֹד עַל זֶה כַּמְבֹאָר לְקַמָּן בְּסוֹף הַפְּתִיחָה, עַיֵּן שָׁם. וּלְבַד זֶה, הֲלוֹא

יָדוּעַ הוּא מִגְּמָרָא דַּעֲרָכִין (טו) הַנַּ"ל שֶׁגָּדֵל הֶעָוֹן הַזֶּה הוּא עַד אֵין

שִׁעוּר, עַד שֶׁאָמְרוּ עָלָיו שֶׁהוּא כְּכוֹפֵר בָּעִקָּר, חַס וְשָׁלוֹם. וְאָמְרוּ

בִּירוּשַׁלְמִי דְּפֵאָה (פרק א׳) שֶׁנִּפְרָעִין מִן הָאָדָם עֲבוּר זֶה הֶעָוֹן בָּעוֹלָם

הַזֶּה וְהַקֶּרֶן קַיֶּמֶת לָעוֹלָם הַבָּא.

See below in the Introduction[a] and in my work *Shemiras Haloshon* where I cite all the statements of the Talmud, the Midrash, and the holy *Zohar* on this matter. If one studies and contemplates them thoroughly, the enormity of this sin will make his hair stand on end.

[Loshon Hora gives strength to the heavenly accusers.]

It seems obvious that the reason why the Torah is so strict about this sin is that it greatly arouses the great Accuser against the Jewish People, and through this he kills many people in many countries. The holy *Zohar* (*Parashas Pekudei* [*p. 264b*]) states:

> There is a certain spiritual being who is in charge of those who are habituated to speak *loshon hora,* and when people arouse themselves to speak *loshon hora,* or when an individual arouses himself to speak *loshon hora,* then that evil, defiled spiritual being, who is called *Sichsucha* (Strife) is aroused in the upper realm, and he rests upon that arousal of *loshon hora* which people initiated, and he comes up above and causes, through that arousal of *loshon hora,* death, war and killing in the world. Woe unto those who arouse this evil aspect, who do not guard their mouth and their tongue and do not

Yad Dovid

a. **in the Introduction:** There *Chofetz Chaim* lists the numerous negative and positive commandments which may be violated when one speaks *loshon hora.*

וְעַיֵּן לְקַמָּן בַּפְּתִיחָה וּבִסְפָרֵי "שְׁמִירַת הַלָּשׁוֹן", שָׁם הֶעְתַּקְנוּ כָּל מַאַמְרֵי הַשַׁ״ס וְהַמִּדְרָשִׁים וְהַזֹּהַר הַקָּדוֹשׁ הַנִּזְכָּרִים בְּעִנְיָן זֶה, וּמִי שֶׁיְּעַיֵּן וְיִתְבּוֹנֵן הֵיטֵב בָּהֶם תִּסָּמַרְנָה שַׂעֲרוֹת רֹאשׁוֹ מִגֹּדֶל הֶעָוֹן.

וְנִרְאֶה פָּשׁוּט, שֶׁהַטַּעַם שֶׁהֶחְמִירָה הַתּוֹרָה כָּל-כַּךְ בְּזֶה הֶעָוֹן – מְשׁוּם שֶׁמְּעוֹרֵר בָּזֶה הַרְבֵּה אֶת הַמְקַטְרֵג הַגָּדוֹל עַל כְּלַל יִשְׂרָאֵל, וְעַל-יְדֵי זֶה הוֹרֵג כַּמָּה אֲנָשִׁים בְּכַמָּה מְדִינוֹת. וְזֶה לְשׁוֹן הַזֹּהַר הַקָּדוֹשׁ פָּרָשַׁת פְּקוּדֵי (דַּף רסד:): אִית רוּחָא חֲדָא דְּקַיְמָא עַל כָּל אִנּוּן מָרֵי דְּלִשָׁנָא בִּישָׁא, דְּכַד מִתְעָרֵי בְּנֵי נָשָׁא בְּלִשָׁנָא בִּישָׁא, אוֹ הַהוּא בַּר נָשׁ דְּאִתְעָרֵי בְּלִשָׁנָא בִּישָׁא, כְּדֵין אִתְעַר הַהוּא רוּחָא בִּישָׁא, מְסָאֲבָא דְּלְעֵלָּא דְּאִקְרֵי סַכְסוּכָא וְאִיהוּ שָׁרֵי עַל הַהוּא אִתְעָרוּתָא דְּלִשָׁנָא בִּישָׁא, דְּשָׁרוּ בֵּהּ בְּנֵי נָשָׁא, וְאִיהוּ עַל לְעֵלָּא וְגָרִים בְּהַהוּא אִתְעָרֵי דְּלִשָׁנָא בִּישָׁא מוֹתָא וְחַרְבָּא וְקִטוּלָא בְּעָלְמָא. וַי לְאִנּוּן דְּמִתְעָרֵי לְהַאי סִטְרָא

pay heed to this, and do not know that the arousal in the upper realms depends upon what is aroused here below whether for good or evil...and all [of the negative forces awakened by the transgression of *loshon hora*] bring accusation in order to awaken that great serpent so that it will bring accusation upon the world. All this is because of that arousal of *loshon hora* which takes place here below.

We can say that this is the intent of the Gemara in *Erachin* [15b, which states:] "Whoever speaks *loshon hora* magnifies his sins up to the heavens, as it is said: 'They set their mouth against heaven, and their tongue struts upon the earth' (*Tehillim* 73:9)." The meaning is: Even though their tongue struts upon the earth, nevertheless their mouth is set against heaven.[a] Likewise *Tanna DeVei Eliyahu*[b] states that the *loshon hora* which a person speaks rises up opposite to the Throne of Glory. From this we can realize the tremendous destruction inflicted upon the Jewish People by habitual speakers of *loshon hora*.

Yad Dovid

a. **set against heaven:** Even though their sin is committed here below, it has effects in the upper realms.

b. **Tanna DeVei Eliyahu:** Eliyahu Rabbah, ch. 18, secs. 124-125 (p. 82 in Shai Lamora edition).

בִּישָׁא וְלָא נָטְרֵי פֻּמַּיְיהוּ וְלִשָּׁנְהוֹן וְלָא חָשְׁשׁוּ עַל דָּא וְלָא יָדְעֵי דְּהָא
בְּאִתְעָרוּתָא דִּלְתַתָּא תַּלְיָא אִתְעָרוּ דִּלְעֵלָּא בֵּין לְטָב בֵּין לְבִישׁ וְכוּ'.
וְכָלְּהוּ דִּילְטוֹרִין לְאִתְעָרָא לְהַאי חִוְיָא רַבָּא לְמֶהֱוֵי הֲלַ טֹרָא עַל עָלְמָא,
וְכָלְּהוּ בְּגִין הַאי אִתְעָרוּ דְּלִשָּׁנָא בִּישָׁא, כַּד קַיְמָא אִתְעָרוּתָא דִּילֵהּ
לְתַתָּא. וְנוּכַל לוֹמַר שֶׁזֶּהוּ כַּוָּנַת הַגְּמָרָא דַּעֲרָכִין הַנַּ"ל: כָּל הַמְסַפֵּר
לָשׁוֹן הָרָע מַגְדִּיל עֲוֹנוֹת עַד לַשָּׁמַיִם, שֶׁנֶּאֱמַר (תהלים עג,ט): שַׁתּוּ
בַשָּׁמַיִם פִּיהֶם וּלְשׁוֹנָם תִּהֲלַךְ בָּאָרֶץ. פֵּרוּשׁ, אַף שֶׁלְּשׁוֹנוֹ הוּא מְהַלֵּךְ
בָּאָרֶץ אֲבָל פִּיו שָׁת בַּשָּׁמַיִם. וְכֵן אִיתָא בְּתָנָא דְּבֵי אֵלִיָּהוּ, שֶׁהַלָּשׁוֹן
הָרָע שֶׁהוּא מְסַפֵּר הוּא עוֹלֶה עַד כְּנֶגֶד כִּסֵּא הַכָּבוֹד, וּמִזֶּה נוּכַל לֵידַע
אֶת גֹּדֶל הַחֻרְבָּן שֶׁמְּחַרִיבִין בַּעֲלֵי הַלָּשׁוֹן אֶת כְּלַל יִשְׂרָאֵל.

[Loshon hora prevents prayer from being heard.]

There is yet another reason for the severity of the damage caused by this sin; for by making a defect in one's speech through forbidden utterances, he impedes all his subsequent holy utterances from rising upwards. These are the words of the holy *Zohar* in *Parashas Pekudei:*

Based upon this evil spiritual being there are a number of other accusers whose task is to seize any bad word or foul word that a person brings forth from his mouth, and [when] he later brings forth holy words woe unto them, woe unto their lives. Woe unto them in this world, woe unto them in the world to come, because these defiled spiritual beings take that defiled word, and when the person later brings forth holy words, those defiled spiritual beings bring that defiled word first, and defile the holy word so that it brings no merit to him, and the strength of the holiness is, as it were, weakened.

Thus we see directly from the holy *Zohar* that all our words of Torah and prayer[a] remain suspended in the air [due to the sin of *loshon hora*] and do not rise upwards. If so, from where will our help come to bring us such things as the coming of *Moshiach?*

When we look deeply into this matter we shall find even more. For besides the fact that it [*loshon hora*] is in itself a grave sin, as explained above, it also causes great destruction in all the [spiritual] worlds, darkening and reducing their light, due to the fact that many people repeatedly violate this

Yad Dovid

a. **Torah and prayer:** This includes the recitation of the *Shema*, the Grace after Meals (*Birkas HaMazon*), and the rest of the hundred blessings we recite each day (*Shemiras HaLoshon*, ch. 16).

וְעוֹד טַעַם אַחֵר לְגֹדֶל הַפְּגַם שֶׁבָּא עַל־יְדֵי עָוֹן זֶה, כִּי עַל־יְדֵי שֶׁאָדָם הוּא פּוֹגֵם אֶת לְשׁוֹנוֹ בְּדִבּוּרִים אֲסוּרִים, הוּא מוֹנֵעַ אַחַר־כָּךְ כָּל דִּבּוּרִים שֶׁל קֹדֶשׁ שֶׁהוּא מְדַבֵּר מִלַּעֲלוֹת לְמַעֲלָה. וְזֶה לְשׁוֹן הַזֹּהַר הַקָּדוֹשׁ פָּרָשַׁת פְּקוּדֵי: וּבְהַאי רוּחָא בִּישָׁא תַּלְיָן כַּמָּה גַּרְדִּינִין אָחֳרָנִין דְּאִנּוּן מְמַנִּין לְאַחֲדָא מִלָּה בִּישָׁא אוֹ מִלָּא טְנוּפָא דְּאַפִּיק בַּר נָשׁ מִפֻּמֵּהּ וּלְבָתַר אַפִּיק מִלִּין קַדִּישִׁין. וַי לוֹן וַי לְחַיֵּיהוֹן וְכוּ'. וַי לוֹן בְּהַאי עָלְמָא וַי לוֹן בְּעָלְמָא דְּאָתֵי. בְּגִין דְּאִלֵּין רוּחִין מְסָאֲבִין נָטְלִין הַהוּא מִלָּא מְסָאֲבָא, וְכַד אַפִּיק בַּר נָשׁ לְבָתַר מִלִּין קַדִּישָׁא, אַקְדִּימִי אִלֵּין רוּחֵי מְסָאֲבָא מִלֵּי הַהוּא מְסָאֲבָא וּמְסָאֲבֵי לְהַהוּא מִלָּה קַדִּישָׁא, וְלָא זָכֵי לֵהּ בַּר נָשׁ, וְכִבְיָכוֹל תָּשְׁשָׁא חֵילָא קַדִּישָׁא, עַד כָּאן לְשׁוֹנוֹ. הֲלוֹא נִרְאֶה בַּעֲלִיל מְזֹהָר הַקָּדוֹשׁ שֶׁכָּל דִּבְרֵי הַתּוֹרָה וּתְפִלָּה שֶׁלָּנוּ הֵם עוֹמְדִים בַּאֲוִיר הַשָּׁמַיִם וְאֵינָם עוֹלִין לְמַעֲלָה, וּמֵאַיִן תָּבוֹא עֶזְרָתֵנוּ לְבִיאַת הַמָּשִׁיחַ וְכַיּוֹצֵא בָזֶה.

וְכַאֲשֶׁר נַעֲמִיק בְּזֶה הָעִנְיָן נִמְצָא עוֹד יוֹתֵר, שֶׁמִּלְּבַד שֶׁהוּא עָוֹן פְּלִילִי בְּעַצְמוֹ וְכַנַּ"ל, עוֹד הוּא מַגְדִּיל הַקִּלְקוּל בְּכָל הָעוֹלָמוֹת

negative precept hundreds and thousands of times during their lifetime; for even a small sin, when repeated many times, eventually becomes "like wagon-ropes," as Isaiah cries out (*Yeshayahu* 5:18): "Alas, those who draw out iniquity with ropes of vanity, and sin [becomes] like wagon-ropes!" The analogy is to silk threads which, when doubled and redoubled hundreds of times, form thick ropes. All the more so does the analogy apply to this sin [of *loshon hora*] which is extremely grave in itself, and many, many people are in the habit of committing it many thousands of times during their lifetime, and they do not accept upon themselves at all to be careful about it certainly the destruction caused to the upper worlds[a] is immeasurable.

[Reasons why people transgress the prohibition of loshon hora]

I have given thought to the question: Why has this negative precept become, in the eyes of many people, so freely open to violation? I realized that this is for a number of reasons with the masses from one standpoint, and with the learned from another standpoint. The masses do not know at all that the prohibition against *loshon hora* applies even to true information. Among the Torah scholars, on the other hand even among those for whom it is clarified and

Yad Dovid

a. **the destruction caused to the upper worlds:** For elucidation of this concept see *Nefesh HaChaim, by R' Chaim* of Volozhin, gate 1, end of ch. 6, and gate 4, end of ch. 25.

וּמַחְשִׁיךְ וּמְמַעֵט אוֹרָן, עַל-יְדֵי שֶׁרְגִילוּת הוּא לְכַמָּה וְכַמָּה אֲנָשִׁים
שֶׁכּוֹפְלִין אֶת הַלָּאו הַזֶּה כַּמָּה מֵאוֹת וַאֲלָפִים פְּעָמִים בִּימֵי חַיֵּיהֶם, כִּי
אֲפִלּוּ עָוֹן קָטָן כְּשֶׁיַּכְפִּיל הַרְבֵּה פְּעָמִים הוּא נַעֲשֶׂה לְבַסּוֹף כַּעֲבוֹת
הָעֲגָלָה, כְּמוֹ שֶׁצָּוַח יְשַׁעְיָה: הוֹי מֹשְׁכֵי הֶעָוֹן בְּחַבְלֵי הַשָּׁוְא וְכַעֲבוֹת
הָעֲגָלָה חַטָּאָה. וְהַמָּשָׁל מֵחוּטֵי הַמֶּשִׁי כְּשֶׁיַּכְפְּלֶנּוּ כַּמָּה מֵאוֹת פְּעָמִים,
וְכָל שֶׁכֵּן בַּחֵטְא הַזֶּה שֶׁהוּא חָמוּר מִצַּד עַצְמוֹ עַד מְאֹד, וּרְגִילִין לַעֲבֹר
עָלָיו הַרְבֵּה וְהַרְבֵּה אֲנָשִׁים בְּכַמָּה אֲלָפִים פְּעָמִים בִּימֵי חַיֵּיהֶם, וְאֵין
מְקַבְּלִין עַל עַצְמָן כְּלָל לְהִשָּׁמֵר מִמֶּנּוּ, שֶׁבְּוַדַּאי הַקִּלְקוּל לְמַעְלָה הוּא
לְאֵין שִׁעוּר.

וָאֶחְשְׁבָה לָדַעַת זֹאת מֵאַיִן נַעֲשָׂה הַלָּאו הַזֶּה הֶפְקֵר כָּל-כָּךְ לְעֵינֵי
הַרְבֵּה בְּנֵי-אָדָם, וְהִתְבּוֹנַנְתִּי שֶׁזֶּה הוּא מִכַּמָּה סִבּוֹת, לֶהָמוֹן מִצַּד אֶחָד
וְלַלּוֹמְדִים מִצַּד אַחֵר. הֶהָמוֹן אֵינָם יוֹדְעִים כְּלָל שֶׁאִסּוּר לָשׁוֹן הָרָע
הוּא אֲפִלּוּ עַל אֱמֶת, וּבַעֲלֵי הַתּוֹרָה – אַף אוֹתָם שֶׁנִּתְבַּרֵר לָהֶם וְנִתְאַמֵּת

verified that the prohibition applies to true information
many are misled by the evil inclination in other ways. For
one, the evil inclination immediately persuades [the scholar]
that the person about whom he wishes to speak is a
hypocrite.[a] The evil inclination tells him: 'It is a mitzvah to
expose hypocrites [b] and wicked people.' Or sometimes [the
evil inclination] tells [the scholar]: "After all, so-and-so is a
quarreler, and [therefore] it is permitted[c] to speak *loshon hora*
about him.' Or sometimes [the evil inclination] entices [the
scholar] with the permission known as "in front of three
people;"[d] or sometimes with the permission known as "in
front of the subject," [meaning] that while relating [the *loshon
hora*] he thinks: 'I would even say this to his face.'[e] And the
evil inclination shows him the relevant Talmud passages. See
below, chs. 2, 3, and 8. Or sometimes [the evil inclination]
entices [the scholar] regarding the nature of the information,
persuading him that it is not in the category of *loshon hora*;
for example many people are accustomed, due to our many
sins, to publicize that someone is not learned; we have
explicated this point below, ch. 5.

Yad Dovid

a. **hypocrite:** This is someone who is wicked but pretends to be righteous
(see *Rashi* to *Yoma* 86b, s.v. מפרסמין and *Hilchos Loshon Hora, Be'er Mayim
Chaim*, ch. 4, clause 30).

b. **It is a mitzvah to expose hypocrites:** For details of this mitzvah see
Yoma there and *Rashi*, loc. cit.

c. **it is permitted:** See *Hilchos Loshon Hora*, ch. 8, clause 8 for details of this
permission.

לָהֶם שֶׁאָסוּר לָשׁוֹן הָרָע אֲפִלּוּ עַל אֱמֶת – יֵשׁ מֵהֶם כַּמָּה שֶׁיֵּצֶר הָרָע
מַטְעֶה אוֹתָם בְּפָנִים אֲחֵרִים. אֶחָד, שֶׁתֵּכֶף מַחְשִׁיב הַיֵּצֶר הָרָע בְּרַעְיוֹנָיו
אֶת הָאִישׁ שֶׁהוּא מְסַפֵּר עָלָיו לְחוֹנֵף, וְאוֹמֵר לוֹ : מִצְוָה לְפַרְסֵם אֶת
הַחֲנֵפִים וְהָרְשָׁעִים. וּפְעָמִים אוֹמֵר לוֹ : הֲלֹא פְּלוֹנִי הוּא בַּעַל-מַחֲלֹקֶת
וּמֻתָּר לְסַפֵּר לָשׁוֹן הָרָע עָלָיו. וְלִפְעָמִים הוּא מְפַתֵּהוּ בְּהֶתֵּרָא דְּאַפֵּי
תְּלָתָא, וּפְעָמִים בְּהֶתֵּרָא דְּאַפֵּי מָרָא, שֶׁמַּסְכִּים בְּעַצְמוֹ בְּעֵת הַסִּפּוּר
שֶׁהָיָה אוֹמֵר לוֹ אַף בְּפָנָיו, וּמְגַלֶּה לוֹ הַיֵּצֶר הָרָע אֶת הַמַּאֲמָרִים הַשַּׁיָּכִים
לָזֶה (וְעַיֵּן לְקַמָּן בִּכְלָל ב' ג' ח'). וּפְעָמִים הוּא מְפַתֵּהוּ בְּאֵיכוּת הַדָּבָר,
לוֹמַר שֶׁאֵין זֶה נִכְנָס בִּכְלָל לָשׁוֹן הָרָע, כְּגוֹן מַה שֶׁרְגִילִין הַרְבֵּה אֲנָשִׁים
בַּעֲווֹנוֹתֵינוּ הָרַבִּים לְפַרְסֵם עַל אֶחָד שֶׁאֵינוֹ חָכָם, וּבֵאַרְנוּ זֶה לְקַמָּן
בִּכְלַל ה'.

Yad Dovid

d. **in front of three people:** This refers to a situation where the
information in question was originally revealed to a group of three or
more listeners. For the details of this permission see *Hilchos Loshon Hora*,
ch. 2.

e. **to his face:** For details of this permission, see *Hilchos Loshon Hora*, ch. 3,
clause 2.

In summary, the evil inclination acts in one of two ways: Either it entices a person to believe that the information he wants to reveal is not in the category of *loshon hora;* or that the person he wants to speak about is not the type about whom the Torah forbids us to speak *loshon hora.*

If the evil inclination sees that it cannot conquer a person with these stratagems, it deceives him in the opposite manner. It presents to him such a strict view of the topic of *loshon hora* as to show him that everything [a person wants to say] is in the category of *loshon hora;* and if so, it is impossible to live upon this earth in this manner, unless he separates himself completely[a] from the matters of this world. This is similar to the slander of the guileful serpent, who said [to Chavah] (*Bereishis* 3:1): "Perhaps God said: 'You shall not eat from *any* tree of the garden?' "[b]

Besides this, many people lack knowledge about the prohibition of believing *loshon hora.* [They do not realize] that even just believing it in one's heart is forbidden, and the only

Yad Dovid

a. **unless he separates himself completely:** This is an attempt on the part of the evil inclination to persuade the person that such a mitzvah is (heaven forbid) too difficult to observe, and therefore the person should give up and allow himself free rein in the area of *loshon hora.* (See *Shemiras HaLoshon, Shaar HaTevunah,* ch. 15.)

כְּלָלוֹ שֶׁל דָּבָר: הַיֵּצֶר הָרָע פְּעֻלָּתוֹ אַחַת מִשְׁתֵּיהֶן, אוֹ שֶׁמְּפַתֵּהוּ שֶׁאֵין דָּבָר זֶה נִכְנָס בִּכְלַל לָשׁוֹן הָרָע, אוֹ שֶׁעַל אִישׁ כָּזֶה לֹא צִוְּתָה הַתּוֹרָה בְּאִסּוּר לָשׁוֹן הָרָע.

וְאִם רוֹאֶה הַיֵּצֶר הָרָע שֶׁבְּאֵלּוּ עִנְיָנִים לֹא יְנַצַּח לָאָדָם, הוּא מְרַמֶּה אוֹתוֹ בְּהֶפֶךְ, שֶׁמַּחְמִיר עָלָיו כָּל-כַּךְ בְּעִנְיָן לָשׁוֹן הָרָע עַד שֶׁמַּרְאֶה לוֹ שֶׁהַכֹּל נִכְנָס בִּכְלַל לָשׁוֹן הָרָע, וְאִם-כֵּן אִי אֶפְשָׁר לִחְיוֹת חַיֵּי תֵּבֵל בְּעִנְיָן זֶה אִם לֹא שֶׁיְּפָרֵשׁ לְגַמְרֵי מֵעִנְיְנֵי הָעוֹלָם, וְהוּא כְּעֵין דִּבַּת הַנָּחָשׁ הֶעָרוּם שֶׁאָמַר: אַף כִּי אָמַר אֱלֹקִים לֹא תֹאכְלוּ מִכָּל עֵץ הַגָּן.

וּלְבַד זֶה, חָסְרָה לְהַרְבֵּה אֲנָשִׁים יְדִיעָה בְּעִנְיָן אִסּוּר קַבָּלַת לָשׁוֹן

Yad Dovid

b. **from any tree of the garden:** He tried to convince her that every tree was forbidden, to make her feel that the commandment was unbearably restrictive.

thing that is permitted is to take any necessary precautions.[a] There are many other similar matters regarding the believing of *loshon hora* and *rechilus* [b] [about which people lack knowledge, but] which cannot be explained here [in this Foreword]. Moreover, people do not know how to make amends [c] if they have transgressed by speaking or believing *loshon hora* or *rechilus.*

For these reasons the matter [of guarding speech] collapses altogether, since inevitably a person falls into the habit of speaking whatever happens to come out of his mouth without thinking first whether his words might be *rechilus* or *loshon hora.* We have become so accustomed to this sin, due to our many iniquities, that because of this many people do not consider it a sin at all, even if someone says something which everyone can clearly see is complete *loshon hora* and *rechilus* for example, if one person speaks evil about another, deprecating him with the utmost derision. If anyone asks him: 'Why did you speak *loshon hora* or *rechilus?*' he will think inwardly: 'He is trying to make me into a saint or a pious one[d],' and will not accept the reprimand at all, since, due to our many sins, he considers this matter as if it were free for everyone to do as he pleases.

Yad Dovid

a. **necessary precautions:** Although it is forbidden to decisively believe the *loshon hora,* one may take precautions to protect oneself in case it might be true (see *Nidah* 61a and *Hilchos Loshon Hora,* ch. 6, clause 10 for details of this permission).

b. *rechilus:* For the definition of *rechilus,* see Overview, sec. 7.

הָרָע, שֶׁאִסּוּרוֹ הוּא אֲפִלּוּ לְהַאֲמִין בַּלֵּב בִּלְבַד, רַק לָחוּשׁ מִבָּעֵי. וְעוֹד
הַרְבֵּה עִנְיָנִים כַּיּוֹצֵא בָזֶה בְּעִנְיָן קַבָּלַת לָשׁוֹן הָרָע וּרְכִילוּת אֲשֶׁר אִי
אֶפְשָׁר לְבָאֲרָם פֹּה. וְאַף אֵינָם יוֹדְעִים אֵיךְ לְתַקֵּן אֶת הַדָּבָר אִם עָבַר עַל
אִסּוּר סִפּוּר לָשׁוֹן הָרָע וּרְכִילוּת וְקַבָּלָתָם.

וּמִצַּד אֵלּוּ הַסִּבּוֹת נִתְמוֹטֵט הָעִנְיָן מִכֹּל וָכֹל, כִּי מִמֵּילָא הָרְגַּל הָאִישׁ
לְדַבֵּר כְּפִי שֶׁיִּזְדַּמֵּן שֶׁיֵּצֵא מִפִּיו, וְלֹא לְהִתְבּוֹנֵן בּוֹ מִתְּחִלָּה פֶּן דָּבָר זֶה
נִכְנָס בִּכְלָל אִסּוּר רְכִילוּת וְלָשׁוֹן הָרָע. וְהֶרְגַּלְנוּ כָּל-כַּךְ בְּעָוֹן זֶה
בְּעֲוֹנוֹתֵינוּ הָרַבִּים עַד שֶׁמִּפְּנֵי זֶה בְּעֵינֵי הַרְבֵּה בְּנֵי-אָדָם אֵין דָּבָר זֶה
נֶחְשָׁב לְעָוֹן כְּלָל, אֲפִלּוּ אִם יְדַבֵּר דָּבָר שֶׁנִּרְאֶה לְכָל שֶׁהוּא לָשׁוֹן הָרָע
וּרְכִילוּת גְּמוּרָה, כְּגוֹן שֶׁהוּא מְדַבֵּר רַע עַל חֲבֵרוֹ וּמְגַנֵּהוּ בְּתַכְלִית
הַגְּנוּת. וְאִם יִשְׁאָלֵהוּ אֶחָד: לָמָה דִּבַּרְתָּ לָשׁוֹן הָרָע אוֹ רְכִילוּת? יַחְשֹׁב
בְּלִבּוֹ שֶׁהוּא בָּא לַעֲשׂוֹתוֹ צַדִּיק וְחָסִיד, וְלֹא יְקַבֵּל אֶת דִּבְרֵי הַמּוֹכִיחַ
כְּלָל בַּאֲשֶׁר שֶׁהוּא רוֹאֶה שֶׁהַדָּבָר הַזֶּה הֶפְקֵר בַּעֲוֹנוֹתֵינוּ הָרַבִּים.

Yad Dovid

c. **how to make amends:** See *Hilchos Loshon Hora*, ch. 4, clause 12, on how
to do *teshuvah* (repent) for speaking *loshon hora*.

d. **a saint or a pious one:** The one who wishes to speak *loshon hora* thinks
he is not violating any basic *halachah*. He thinks the one reproving him is
trying to make him conform to *midas chassidus*, the standards of
extraordinary pious people. (See below, p. 86 where *Chofetz Chaim*
emphasizes: "I did not write this work according to *midas chassidus*...".

[The need for a book on the laws of loshon hora]

All these reasons [why the evil inclination is able to entice people to speak *loshon hora*] can be traced to the fact that there is no single work where the topic of *loshon hora* and *rechilus* is dealt with comprehensively, clarifying the definition of these prohibitions and their ramifications, both in general principle and specific detail. Rather, these matters are scattered in various places in the Talmud and the works of the *Rishonim* [early authorities]. Even *Rambam* (in *Hilchos De'os,* ch. 7) and Rabbeinu Yonah (in *Shaarei Teshuvah*[a]), who paved the way for us regarding these laws [by giving an overall survey of the topic], nevertheless were extremely brief, as is the way of the *Rishonim.* In addition, there are many laws which they do not mention at all, as the reader will see in this present work.

Therefore I have girded myself like a man of action and with the help of Hashem, Blessed be He, Who graciously endows man with wisdom, I have collected all the laws of *loshon hora* and *rechilus* into a book. I have gleaned these laws from all the scattered places in the Talmud and *Poskim* [halachic authorities] in particular from *Rambam, Sefer Mitzvos Gadol,* and *Shaarei Teshuvah* by Rabbeinu Yonah of blessed memory, all of whom have illuminated our eyes in these *halachos.* I have also included certain laws which I found in the responsa of *Maharik,*[b] as well as other pertinent responsa.

Yad Dovid

a. in *Shaarei Teshuvah:* Ch. 2, clause 200 ff.

וְכָל אֵלּוּ הַסִּבּוֹת עִקָּרָם הוּא מִצַּד שֶׁלֹּא נִתְקַבֵּץ בְּמָקוֹם אֶחָד עִנְיַן
לָשׁוֹן הָרָע וּרְכִילוּת, שֶׁיִּתְבָּאֵר בּוֹ אֵיכוּתָם וְעִנְיָנָם בִּכְלָלֵיהֶם וּפְרָטֵיהֶם,
אֲבָל הֵם מְפֻזָּרִים בְּשַׁ"ס וְרִאשׁוֹנִים; וַאֲפִלּוּ הָרַמְבַּ"ם בְּפֶרֶק ז' מֵהִלְכוֹת
דֵּעוֹת וְרַבֵּנוּ יוֹנָה בְּשַׁעֲרֵי-תְשׁוּבָה, שֶׁהֵם עָשׂוּ לָנוּ דֶּרֶךְ סְלוּלָה בַּהֲלָכָה
זוֹ, אַף-עַל-פִּי-כֵן קַצְּרוּ מְאֹד כְּדַרְכָּן שֶׁל רִאשׁוֹנִים, וְגַם יֵשׁ הַרְבֵּה
וְהַרְבֵּה דִינִים שֶׁלֹּא בָא בְּדִבְרֵיהֶן כַּאֲשֶׁר יִרְאֶה הָרוֹאֶה בִּפְנִים הַסֵּפֶר.

עַל כֵּן אָזַרְתִּי כְּגֶבֶר חֲלָצַי בְּעֶזְרַת הַשֵּׁם יִתְבָּרַךְ הַחוֹנֵן לְאָדָם דַּעַת,
וְקִבַּצְתִּי כָּל דִּינֵי לָשׁוֹן הָרָע וּרְכִילוּת אֶל סֵפֶר, וְלִקַּטְתִּי אוֹתָם מִכָּל
הַמְּקוֹמוֹת הַמְפֻזָּרִים בַּשַׁ"ס וּבַפּוֹסְקִים, וּבִפְרָט מֵהָרַמְבַּ"ם וְהַסְּמַ"ג
וְהַשַּׁעֲרֵי-תְשׁוּבָה לְרַבֵּנוּ יוֹנָה ז"ל, שֶׁהֵם הֵאִירוּ לָנוּ הָעֵינַיִם בַּהֲלָכָה זוֹ,
וְגַם לִקַּטְתִּי אֵיזֶה דִינִים מִמַּה שֶׁמְּצָאתִי בִּתְשׁוּבַת מַהֲרִי"ק וּשְׁאָרֵי
תְּשׁוּבוֹת הַשַׁיָּכִים לְעִנְיָן זֶה.

Yad Dovid

b. ***Maharik:*** R' Yosef Colon (1410-1480), a major halachic authority of both
Italian and Ashkenazic Jewry.

[The structure of this book]

I have divided the work into two parts: 1. *The Laws of Loshon Hora.* 2. *The Laws of Rechilus.*

NOTE:[a]
The truth is that there are many laws of *rechilus* which can be logically inferred from the laws of *loshon hora.* However I decided that it is necessary to repeat every single law in detail, [b] due to the great stumbling-block presented by this sin of speech, may the Merciful One save us. When the reader is studying our work for practical application it would not be right to expect him to seek out and deduce one law from another, exhausting all the possible interpretations. Moreover, in almost every single topic [in the laws of *rechilus*] there is some new point which we cannot infer from the laws of *loshon hora.* In this vein the Sages said (*Sotah* 3a): "Whenever a passage [of the Torah] is repeated, it is only repeated for the sake of something new[c] that appears in it."
Yad Dovid

a. **NOTE:** The following appears in the original work as a footnote.

b. **to repeat every single law in detail:** Even where it is logically evident that a particular law regarding *loshon hora* applies also to *rechilus,* I decided to state the law again in *Hilchos Rechilus.*

וְחִלַּקְתִּי אֶת הַסֵּפֶר לִשְׁנֵי חֲלָקִים: א. הִלְכוֹת אִסּוּרֵי לָשׁוֹן הָרָע; ב. הִלְכוֹת אִסּוּרֵי רְכִילוּת.

הגה"ה

וּבֶאֱמֶת יֵשׁ הַרְבֵּה דִינִים בְּהִלְכוֹת רְכִילוּת שֶׁנּוּכַל לִלְמֹד אוֹתָם מִדִּינֵי אִסּוּרֵי לָשׁוֹן הָרָע, אַךְ אָמַרְתִּי הַהֶכְרֵחַ לַחֲזֹר עוֹד כָּל דִין וָדִין בִּפְרָטִיּוּת מֵחֲמַת גֹּדֶל הַמִּכְשׁוֹל הַמָּצוּי בָּזֶה הַחֵטְא, חֵטְא הַלָּשׁוֹן, רַחֲמָנָא לִצְלַן, וְאֵין לִסְמֹךְ בְּעִנְיָן כָּזֶה עַל הַמְעַיֵּן שֶׁכַּאֲשֶׁר יִהְיֶה צָרִיךְ לְאֵיזֶה דָבָר לְמַעֲשֶׂה יְחַפֵּשׂ לִלְמֹד דָבָר מִתּוֹךְ דָּבָר, וְכַלֵּה הַאי וְאוּלַי. גַּם שֶׁכִּמְעַט בְּכָל עִנְיָן וְעִנְיָן יֵשׁ אֵיזֶה הִתְחַדְּשׁוּת אֲשֶׁר לֹא נוּכַל לִלְמֹד זֶה מִדִּינֵי אִסּוּרֵי לָשׁוֹן הָרָע, וּכְבָר אָמְרוּ חַז"ל בְּכַיּוֹצֵא בָּזֶה: כָּל פָּרָשָׁה שֶׁנֶּאֶמְרָה וְנִשְׁנֵית, לֹא נִשְׁנֵית אֶלָּא בִּשְׁבִיל דָּבָר שֶׁנִּתְחַדֵּשׁ בָּהּ.

Yad Dovid

c. **for the sake of something new:** That is, the Torah sometimes repeats certain words that contain no innovation, in order to lead up to an innovation (see the Gemara there). Similarly in the Laws of *Rechilus* the author repeats certain laws applying to *loshon hora* in order to lead up to innovations regarding *rechilus*.

83

(If the Supernal One will give me the merit, I shall see to it this is not a vow to join to these two parts [*Hilchos Loshon Hora* and *Hilchos Rechilus*] a third part,[a] in which will be collected all the statements of the Gemara, the Midrash and the holy *Zohar* on this topic; and this will make clear the tremendous reward, in this world and in the world to come, for someone who is careful to avoid this sin, and the severity of the punishment for anyone who transgresses it.)

Afterwards I divided the aforementioned laws into chapters, and each chapter into a number of clauses, for ease of reading. In almost every chapter I provided relevant concrete examples so that the reader will understand how to be careful about these matters in practice.

I have called this work *Chofetz Chaim* [literally, "Desires Life"], alluding to the verse [*Tehillim* 34:13-14]: "Who is the man who *desires life?*... [Guard your tongue from evil.]" So that the reader should not become weary in reading every law along with its sources, since sometimes [the explanation of the sources] is very lengthy, I divided [the exposition] in two: [1] the main text, presenting in brief the law which emerges after examination of all the source material. This part is called *Mekor HaChaim* (*The Source of Life*), because man's speech comes from the power of the living soul within him, as we see from the verse: "Man became a living soul" (*Bereishis* 2:7), which Onkelos renders: "...a speaking soul." [2] The accompanying explanation, which is called *Be'er Mayim Chaim* (*Well of Living Waters*) because it is the wellspring from which I drew the main text, *The Source of Life*.

Yad Dovid

a. **a third part:** This refers to the ethical work *Shemiras HaLoshon*.

(וְכַאֲשֶׁר יְזַכֵּנִי הָעֶלְיוֹן, אֶרְאֶה – בְּלִי נֶדֶר – לְחַבֵּר אֶל אֵלּוּ שְׁנֵי הַחֲלָקִים עוֹד חֵלֶק שְׁלִישִׁי, אֲשֶׁר בּוֹ יְקַבֵּץ כָּל הַמַּאֲמָרִים הַנִּזְכָּרִים בִּגְמָרָא וּמִדְרָשִׁים וְזֹהַר הַקָּדוֹשׁ מֵעִנְיָן זֶה, כִּי מִתּוֹךְ זֶה יְבֹאַר עֶצֶם הַשָּׂכָר בָּעוֹלָם הַזֶּה וּבָעוֹלָם הַבָּא לְמִי שֶׁנִּזְהָר מֵעָוֹן זֶה וְגֹדֶל הָעֹנֶשׁ לְמִי שֶׁעוֹבֵר עַל זֶה.) וְאַחַר-כָּךְ חִלַּקְתִּי אֶת הַהֲלָכוֹת הַנַּ"ל לִכְלָלִים, וְכָל כְּלָל – לְכַמָּה סְעִיפִים, כְּדֵי שֶׁיָּרוּץ הַקּוֹרֵא בּוֹ. וְכִמְעַט בְּכָל כְּלָל צִיַּרְתִּי אֵיזֶה צִיּוּרִים הַשַּׁיָּכִים לִכְלָל זֶה, כְּדֵי שֶׁמִּמֶּנּוּ יִתְבּוֹנֵן הַקּוֹרֵא אֵיךְ לִזָּהֵר בָּזֶה לְמַעֲשֶׂה.

וְקָרָאתִי אֶת שֵׁם הַסֵּפֶר הַזֶּה בִּכְלָלוֹ חָפֵץ חַיִּים עַל שֵׁם הַכָּתוּב: מִי הָאִישׁ הֶחָפֵץ חַיִּים וְכוּ'. וּמִפְּנֵי שֶׁלֹּא יָקוּץ הַקּוֹרֵא בִּקְרִיאָתוֹ כָּל דִּין וּמְקוֹרוֹ מֵחֲמַת רֹב הָאֲרִיכוּת שֶׁנִּמְצָא בּוֹ לִפְעָמִים, עַל-כֵּן חִלַּקְתִּיו לִשְׁנַיִם: הַפְּנִים, וְהוּא הַהֲלָכָה בְּקִצּוּר הַיּוֹצֵאת אַחַר בֵּרוּר כָּל הַדְּבָרִים, יִקָּרֵא בְּשֵׁם מְקוֹר הַחַיִּים, כִּי הַדִּבּוּר שֶׁבָּאָדָם הוּא יוֹצֵא מִכֹּחַ נֶפֶשׁ הַחַיָּה אֲשֶׁר בּוֹ, וּכְמוֹ שֶׁכָּתוּב: וַיְהִי הָאָדָם לְנֶפֶשׁ חַיָּה, וְתִרְגֵּם אֻנְקְלוֹס: לְרוּחַ מְמַלְּלָא. וּבֵאוּר סָבִיב לוֹ יִקָּרֵא בְּשֵׁם בְּאֵר מַיִם חַיִּים, כִּי הוּא הַבְּאֵר שֶׁדָּלִיתִי מִמֶּנּוּ אֶת מְקוֹר הַחַיִּים הַפְּנִימִי.

My brother the reader should be aware that for every law mentioned in *Mekor HaChaim*, even obvious ones, I have cited the sources in *Be'er Mayim Chaim*, so that it will be clear to the eyes of all that I did not write this work in accord with practices of extraordinary piety; on the contrary, I only present here what is required by the basic law.

[A request to the reader]

I beseech the pleasant reader perhaps he will find something that does not seem correct to him at first glance. It might be the law itself, which he thinks is merely a non-essential stringency; or he might think I have treated some topic with unnecessary elaboration, or too briefly. Let him not hurry to decide that it is an error, until he has thoroughly studied *Be'er Mayim Chaim* and all the general principles applicable to the law in question. For if he overlooks even one general principle regarding this law he will not properly understand the rest of the law. The truth is that I have devoted much study to every single paragraph of this work (in close consultation with great Torah scholars), and have searched again and again to make sure that nothing in the Talmud contradicts our words. In many instances I studied a single question for many days until I clarified the true halachah, with the help of Hashem, Blessed be He.

I hope to Hashem, Blessed be He, that if the reader listens to these words and thoroughly studies all the general prin-

וְיֵדַע אָחִי הַקּוֹרֵא, שֶׁאֲפִלּוּ כָּל דָּבָר פָּשׁוּט שֶׁנִּמְצָא בִּפְנִים הֶרְאֵיתִי אֶת
מְקוֹרוֹ בִּבְאֵר מַיִם חַיִּים, לְמַעַן יְבֹרַר לְעֵינֵי הַכֹּל שֶׁסֵּפֶר זֶה לֹא חִבַּרְתִּי
עַל-פִּי מִדַּת חֲסִידוּת רַק עַל צַד הַדִּין.

(וְאֲחַלֶּה לַקּוֹרֵא הַנָּעִים, אוּלַי יִצְמָא אֵיזֶה דָּבָר שֶׁלֹּא יִהְיֶה נִרְאֶה לוֹ
בְּהַשְׁקָפָה רִאשׁוֹנָה – אִם בְּעֶצֶם הַדִּין, כִּי יֹאמַר שֶׁהוּא חַמְרָא בְּעָלְמָא,
אוֹ אֲרִיכוּת הַלָּשׁוֹן לְלֹא צֹרֶךְ, אוֹ קִצּוּר לָשׁוֹן – בַּל יְמַהֵר לְהַחְלִיט אֶת
הַדָּבָר לוֹמַר שְׁגָגָה הִיא עַד אֲשֶׁר יְעַיֵּן הֵיטֵב בַּבְּאֵר מַיִם חַיִּים וּבְכָל
הַכְּלָלִים הַנִּצְרָכִים לְהַהֲלָכָה זוֹ, כִּי אַף אִם יֶחְסַר לוֹ כְּלָל אֶחָד מֵהֲלָכָה זוֹ
לֹא יָבִין שְׁאָר הַהֲלָכָה לַאֲשׁוּרוֹ. כִּי בֶּאֱמֶת כָּל סָעִיף וְסָעִיף מִסֵּפֶר הַזֶּה
עִיַּנְתִּי בּוֹ הַרְבֵּה (וּבְדִבּוּק חֲבֵרִים גְּדוֹלֵי הַתּוֹרָה), וְחִפַּשְׂתִּי חִפּוּשׂ אַחַר
חִפּוּשׂ שֶׁלֹּא יִמָּצֵא בַּשַּׁ"ס סְתִירָה לִדְבָרֵינוּ. וְכַמָּה פְּעָמִים עִיַּנְתִּי בְּעִנְיָן
אֶחָד כַּמָּה יָמִים, עַד שֶׁבֵּרַרְתִּי הַהֲלָכָה לַאֲמִתָּהּ בְּעֶזְרַת הַשֵּׁם יִתְבָּרַךְ.

87

ciples of the halachah 'his eyes will see honest laws,'[a] for every single word in the main text of this work was written with meticulous attention to the law. At times I could have changed the wording [of certain matters], phrasing them more briefly or more elaborately, so that the intent would be more easily understood. However I did not wish to depart from the wording of *Rambam* and other *Poskim* who are the source of the law. Whoever judges me on the side of merit, the Omnipresent will judge him on the side of merit.

NOTE:

The reader should not be puzzled by the question: Since the underlying principle of this entire work is to set forth the basic laws, why do I cite proofs in a number of places from *Shaarei Teshuvah* by Rabbeinu Yonah, which is a work of *Mussar?*[b] For in truth anyone who properly examines that author's holy statements in a number of places will see clearly that he meticulously guarded his words to keep them within the confines of the basic law. This is particularly true in his Laws of *Loshon Hora*. For every single matter on which he

Yad Dovid

a. **his eyes will see honest laws:'** The phrase is based on *Tehillim* 17:2.

88

וַאֲקַוֶּה לְהַשֵּׁם יִתְבָּרַךְ כִּי הַקּוֹרֵא אֲשֶׁר יִשְׁמַע לִדְבָרֵינוּ אֵלֶּה וִיעַיֵּן הֵיטֵב
בְּכָל כְּלָלֵי הַהֲלָכָה, עֵינָיו יֶחֱזוּ מֵישָׁרִים כִּי כָּל מִלָּה וּמִלָּה שֶׁבִּפְנִים
הַסֵּפֶר נִכְתְּבָה בִּדְקְדּוּק הַדִּין. וְלִפְעָמִים הָיָה בִּיכָלְתִּי לְשַׁנּוֹת אֶת
הַלָּשׁוֹן, לְקַצֵּר אוֹ לְהַאֲרִיךְ, לְמַעַן יִהְיֶה נָקֵל לְהָבִין הַמְכֻוָּן בּוֹ, אוּלָם לֹא
רָצִיתִי לְשַׁנּוֹת לְשׁוֹן הָרַמְבַּ"ם וּשְׁאָרֵי פּוֹסְקִים שֶׁהַדִּין נוֹבֵעַ מֵהֶם. וְכָל
אֲשֶׁר יְדִינֵנִי לְכַף זְכוּת, הַמָּקוֹם יְדִינֵהוּ לְכַף זְכוּת).

הגה"ה

וְאַל יִפָּלֵא בְּעֵינֵי הַקּוֹרֵא: כֵּיָן שֶׁכָּל הַסֵּפֶר הַזֶּה
הוּא מְיֻסָּד עַל עִקְרֵי הַהֲלָכָה, לָמָה אֲנִי מֵבִיא
בְּכַמָּה מְקוֹמוֹת רְאָיוֹת מִסֵּפֶר "שַׁעֲרֵי- תְשׁוּבָה"
לְרַבֵּנוּ יוֹנָה, שֶׁהוּא מִכְּלַל סִפְרֵי מוּסָר. כִּי בֶּאֱמֶת
נִרְאָה לָעֵינַיִם לַמִּתְבּוֹנֵן הֵיטֵב בְּמַאֲמָרָיו הַקְּדוֹשִׁים
בְּכַמָּה מְקוֹמוֹת, שֶׁשָּׁמַר וְדִקְדֵּק אֶת דְּבָרָיו שֶׁלֹּא
יֵצֵא מִגֶּדֶר הַדִּין, וּבִפְרָט בְּדִינֵי לָשׁוֹן הָרָע שֶׁלּוֹ

Yad Dovid

b. **mussar.** *Chofetz Chaim* stated above (p. 86) that his work was not written
in accord with practices of extraordinary piety, but presents only the basic
law. Works of *Mussar*, on the other hand, usually are designed partly, or
even primarily, to help the reader achieve extraordinary piety.

every single matter on which he wrote, there is a source in the Talmud, as we shall make clear, God willing, in the body of our work. However, he wrote in a very concise style, without indicating his sources, as was the way of the *Rishonim*. All the same, in most instances I did not base my ruling upon him alone, except where his words imply a leniency of some kind. (I followed the same rule with other works of *Mussar*.) But wherever a stringency was involved I almost always gave other sources [in addition to *Shaarei Teshuvah*], as will be evident to anyone who studies our text.

[Possible abuse of this work]

I know there may be people whose will and desire is to find fault with their fellow Jews, and who have so habituated themselves to this bitter sin that nothing will help turn them back from their evil way. People of this sort, upon finding some leniency in my book, will not be at all meticulous about the details upon which [the leniency] depends, and thus will permit many things which I never intended. Nor will their conscience trouble

בְּכָל עִנְיָן וְעִנְיָן שֶׁכָּתַב יֵשׁ עַל זֶה מָקוֹרמִן הַשַׁ"ס (וְכַאֲשֶׁר נְבָאֵר, אִם יִרְצֶה הַשֵּׁם, בִּפְנִים הַסֵּפֶר), אַךְ הוּא קָצֵר מְאֹד וְלֹא הֵבִיא אֶת הַמְּקוֹרוֹת כְּדַרְכָּן שֶׁל רִאשׁוֹנִים, וּבְכָל זֹאת עַל-פִּי הָרֹב לֹא סָמַכְתִּי עָלָיו לְבַד רַק בְּמָקוֹם שֶׁנִּשְׁמָע מִדְּבָרָיו אֵיזֶה קַלָּא (וְכֵן כְּהַאי גַוְנָא מִשְּׁאָר סִפְרֵי מוּסָר), אֲבָל לַחֲמָרָא כִּמְעַט רֻבּוֹ כְּכֻלּוֹ הֵבֵאתִי עוֹד אֵיזֶה רְאָיוֹת, כַּאֲשֶׁר יִרְאֶה הַמְעַיֵּן בִּפְנִים.

וְיוֹדֵעַ אֲנִי, כִּי יוּכַל לִהְיוֹת שֶׁיִּמְצְאוּ אֲנָשִׁים שֶׁרְצוֹנָם וּתְשׁוּקָתָם לָתֵן דֹּפִי בְּחַבְרֵיהֶם, וְהִרְגִּילוּ אֶת עַצְמָם בְּעָוֹן הַמַּר הַזֶּה עַד אֲשֶׁר לֹא יוֹעִיל לָהֶם שׁוּם דָּבָר לַהֲשִׁיבָם מִדַּרְכָּם הָרָעָה, וְאֲנָשִׁים כָּאֵלוּ כַּאֲשֶׁר יִמְצְאוּ בְּסִפְרִי זֶה אֵיזֶה קַלָּא לֹא יְדַקְדְּקוּ כְּלָל בַּפְּרָטִים הַנִּצְרָכִים לָזֶה וְיַתִּירוּ עַל-יְדֵי זֶה כַּמָּה דְּבָרִים אֲשֶׁר לֹא עָלְתָה עַל לִבִּי, וְלֹא יִהְיֶה

91

them about this, for they will claim to be following this book. Nevertheless I decided that it would not be right, because of people like these, to withhold good from those who are sincere. Similarly the Sages said in *Bava Basra* [89b]: "He spoke of them,[a] and it was on the basis of this verse that he spoke of them: 'The ways of Hashem are straight; the righteous will walk upon them and sinners will stumble upon them'[b] (*Hoshea* 14:10).

[Would it be better to leave people ignorant?]

I know full well that there will be people who will want to belittle the value of studying this matter [the laws of *loshon hora*]. They will base themselves upon the saying of the Sages (*Shabbos* 148b): "It is

Yad Dovid

a. **He spoke of them:** The Gemara there discusses certain fraudulent trade practices, such as dishonest weights. Rabban Yochanan ben Zakkai was in a dilemma as to whether he should lecture on these practices. "Woe to me if I speak of them, woe to me if I do not speak of them. If I speak of them, swindlers might learn them…". The Gemara explains how he resolved the dilemma: "He spoke of them…".

גַּם-כֵּן לְבַם נוֹקְפָם עַל זֶה כִּי יִתְלוּ בַּסֵּפֶר הַזֶּה; אַךְ אָמַרְתִּי לֹא אֶמְנַע טוֹב לְהוֹלְכִים בְּתָמִים בִּשְׁבִיל אֲנָשִׁים כָּאֵלוּ, כְּמוֹ שֶׁאָמְרוּ חַז"ל בְּאֹפֶן כָּזֶה בְּבָבָא בַּתְרָא (פט:): אֲמָרָה, וּמֵהַאי קְרָא אֲמָרָה (הושע יד, י): כִּי יְשָׁרִים דַּרְכֵי ה' צַדִּיקִים יֵלְכוּ בָם וְכוּ'.

וְיָדַעְתִּי גַּם יָדַעְתִּי, כִּי יִמָּצְאוּ אֲנָשִׁים אֲשֶׁר יִרְצוּ לְהַמְעִיט אֶת מַעֲלַת הַלִּמוּד בְּעִנְיָן זֶה וְיִתְלוּ אֶת עַצְמָן בְּמַאֲמַר חַז"ל: מוּטָב שֶׁיִּהְיוּ שׁוֹגְגִין וְאַל יִהְיוּ מְזִידִין.

Yad Dovid

b. **sinners will stumble upon them:** Even though sinners will use Torah to justify their misdeeds, that is no reason to withhold Torah from the righteous.

preferable that they should [sin] in ignorance
and not [sin] knowingly."[a] But the truth is that I
am right [to inform people about these laws],
for two reasons: (1) The rule, "It is preferable
that they should [sin] in ignorance…" does not
apply to commandments which are stated
explicitly in the Torah, as [Shulchan Aruch] rules
in Orach Chaim [608:2 in the Hagoh] and [the
prohibition against] loshon hora and rechilus are
stated explicitly in the Torah.[b] Moreover, if it
were true [that we should not inform people of
prohibitions that are difficult for them to
observe], then we should not teach the laws of
theft in public, since they too are very difficult
to observe, as the Sages noted in Bava Basra
[165a].[c]

Yad Dovid

a. **and not sin knowingly:** In a case where it is known that a prohibition is
difficult to observe, and even if informed of it the people will go on
violating it, it is better not to inform them, so that they will only incur the
lesser punishment for violating it through ignorance rather than the
greater punishment for violating it knowingly. (And see *Beitzah* 30a and
Rashi there, s.v. מוטב.)

b. **explicitly in the Torah:** Several verses refer to the prohibition against
loshon hora, as explained below, *Hilchos Loshon Hora*, ch. 1, *Be'er Mayim
Chaim*, clause 4. And *rechilus* is explicitly prohibited in *Vayikra* 19:16.

אַךְ בֶּאֱמֶת הַדִּין אִתִּי מִצְדֵּי צְדָדִים: א. בְּדָבָר
הַמְפֹרָשׁ בַּתּוֹרָה אֵין אוֹמְרִים מוּטָב וְכוּ', כְּמוֹ
שֶׁפָּסַק בְּאֹרַח-חַיִּים בְּסִימָן תר"ח סְעִיף ב' בְּהַגָּ"ה,
וְלָשׁוֹן הָרָע וּרְכִילוּת הוּא דָבָר הַמְפֹרָשׁ בַּתּוֹרָה.
וְעוֹד, אִם-כֵּן לֹא נְלַמֵּד לָרַבִּים הִלְכוֹת גָּזֵל, דְּגַם זֶה
קָשֶׁה מְאֹד לְקַיֵּם כְּמוֹ שֶׁאָמְרוּ חַז"ל בְּבָבָא בַּתְרָא
(קסה).

(וְאַף שֶׁבִּלְשׁוֹן הָרָע אָמְרוּ שָׁם שֶׁכֻּלָּם נִכְשָׁלִין,

Yad Dovid

c. in **Bava Basra** 165a: Rav Yehudah said in the name of Rav: "Most people [are suspect] of theft." (See *Rashi* there, s.v. רוב בגזל for the explanation.) Nevertheless we do teach the laws of theft to the public. Hence we should likewise teach the laws of *loshon hora*.

(True, the Gemara says there that everyone is guilty of *loshon hora.*[a] However, this refers only to *avak loshon hora,*[b] as we see from the Gemara's objection there: "Do you think [everyone is guilty of actual] *loshon hora?*" Thus the study of these matters can at least save people from the sin itself.[c] But [in fact] a person can be saved even from *avak loshon hora* if he puts his heart and mind to it, for when the Gemara [*Bava Basra* 164b] said, "No one is saved from... [*avak*] *loshon hora,*" it only meant in the average case.)[d]

Likewise [if it were true that we should not inform people of prohibitions that are difficult to observe] we should not teach people the laws of the Sabbath, which are

Yad Dovid

a. **everyone is guilty of *loshon hora:*** Thus it might seem that the prohibition of *loshon hora* is even more difficult to observe than that of theft, and therefore we should not inform people about it, since this will only change them from unknowing to knowing transgressors.

b. **avak loshon hora:** For the definition see Overview, sec. 6.

c. **the sin itself:** Even if it will not save people from *avak loshon hora,* which the Gemara says everyone commits, it will save them from *loshon hora* itself.

הֲלוֹא לֹא אָמְרוּ רַק בְּאָבָק, כְּמוֹ שֶׁהִקְשָׁה הַגְּמָרָא
שָׁם: בִּלְשׁוֹן הָרַע סָלְקָא דַּעְתָּךְ ?! וְיִהְיֶה תּוֹעֶלֶת
עַל-כָּל-פָּנִים מִלְּמוּד עִנְיָנִים אֵלּוּ לְהִנָּצֵל מֵעֶצֶם
הֶעָוֹן. וַאֲפִלּוּ מֵאֲבַק לָשׁוֹן הָרַע יוּכַל לְהִנָּצֵל אִם
יִתֵּן לִבּוֹ וְרַעְיוֹנָיו לָזֶה, דְּלֹא אָמְרוּ: אֵין אָדָם וְכוּ'
רַק בִּסְתָמָא.)

וְכֵן לֹא נִלְמְדֶם הִלְכוֹת שַׁבָּת שֶׁהֵם כַּהֲרָרִים

Yad Dovid

d. **in the average case:** The Gemara was speaking of the average case, where the person is not making a conscious effort to avoid the sin. But if one puts his heart and mind to it, he can avoid it. Thus even regarding *avak loshon hora* we should not say: "It is preferable that they should [sin] in ignorance…"

97

"like mountains hanging from a hair,"[a] and
which include many laws which are very
difficult to observe.[b]

Furthermore [if it were true that the
laws of *loshon hora* should not be taught to
the public], why did the Sages in *Erachin*
[15b-16a] publicize the main principles of
these matters, as when they said there:
"What [kind of a statement] constitutes
loshon hora? 'There is fire in so-and-so's
house.' "[c] And similar teachings [about the
principles of *loshon hora* are found in the
Gemara there]. Moreover, we can prove
from Scripture itself [that the laws of *loshon
hora* should be taught to the public], for it is
written in the Torah (*Devorim* 24:9):
"Remember what Hashem your God did to
Miriam," and *Ramban* says in the name of
Sifri that this means one must regularly
make verbal mention of the story of
Miriam [who was punished with leprosy
for speaking disparagingly about Moshe
Rabbeinu], so that through this
[remembrance of Miriam] we should
contemplate the gravity of this bitter sin.

Yad Dovid

a. **"mountains hanging from a hair:"** Mishnah in *Chagigah* 10a. The
Mishnah means that many weighty laws of the Sabbath are derived from
very slight hints in the Torah (*Rashi* there). *Chofetz Chaim's* point is that
many laws of very serious consequence depend upon subtle reasoning
and are thus difficult to understand and remember.

b. **difficult to observe:** Even when one understands them he must exert
effort to fulfill them.

הַתְּלוּיִים בְּשַׁעֲרָה, וְהַרְבֵּה דִינִים יֵשׁ בָּהֶם שֶׁקָּשֶׁה
מְאֹד לְקַיֵּם אוֹתָם. וְעוֹד, אֵיךְ הֶעְתִּיקוּ לָנוּ חֲזַ"ל
בַּעֲרָכִין (טו: ; טז) הָעִקָּרִים בְּעִנְיָנִים אֵלּוּ, כְּגוֹן מַה
שֶּׁאָמְרוּ שָׁם: הֵיכִי דָּמִי לִשָּׁנָא בִּישָׁא? נוּרָא בֵּי
פְּלָנְיָא, וְכַדּוֹמֶה. וְעוֹד, מִגּוּפָא דְּקְרָא נוֹכִיחַ: הֲלוֹא
כְּתִיב בַּתּוֹרָה: זָכוֹר אֵת אֲשֶׁר עָשָׂה ה' אֱלֹהֶיךָ
לְמִרְיָם וְכוּ', וְהֵבִיא הָרַמְבַּ"ן בְּבֵאוּרוֹ בְּשֵׁם הַסִּפְרִי
שֶׁצָּרִיךְ לִזְכֹּר תָּמִיד בַּפֶּה מַעֲשֵׂה מִרְיָם כְּדֵי

Yad Dovid

c. **"There is fire in so-and-so's house:"** "Where is there fire [in the oven at this hour] except in so-and-so's house, where there is always fish and meat [being cooked]" implying that the householder is over-indulgent (Gemara there).

But according to their argument [those
who say these laws should not be taught
because people in any case will not observe
them] on the contrary, we should not
remember [what Hashem did to Miriam],
and thus we could remain unknowing
transgressors of this [sin]! But certainly the
Torah comprehended the mind of man and
knew that it is within his power to be
careful about this sin. If it were otherwise
[it would contradict the principle that]
"The Holy One, Blessed is He does not deal
tyrannically with His creatures" [i.e., He
does not punish them for something they
could never have fulfilled; *Avodah Zarah*
3a]. But in fact if one regularly
contemplates this[a] it undoubtedly will help
him greatly to be saved from this sin.

*[Learning the laws of loshon hora will at least
keep a person from falling into the category of
baalei loshon hora.]*

There is another great benefit to be
gained from the study of these matters [of
loshon hora, namely] that as a result of this
[study] it will not appear to him as an area
where everyone is free to do as he pleases.
Then even if, heaven forbid, he
occasionally stumbles in this offense, he

Yad Dovid

a. **if one regularly contemplates this:** If one regularly thinks about the
laws of loshon hora, for example by contemplating what happened to
Miriam.

שֶׁעַל-יְדֵי זֶה נִתְבּוֹנֵן אֶת גֹּדֶל הֶעָוֹן הַמַּר,
וּלְדִבְרֵיהֶם אַדְּרַבָּה לֹא נִזְכֹּר וְנוּכַל לִהְיוֹת שׁוֹגְגִין
בָּזֶה, אֶלָּא וַדַּאי דְּהַתּוֹרָה יָרְדָה לְסוֹף דַּעַת הָאָדָם
שֶׁבְּכֹחוֹ לִהְיוֹת נִזְהָר מִזֶּה הֶעָוֹן (דְּאִי לָאו הָכֵי אֵין
הַקָּדוֹשׁ-בָּרוּךְ-הוּא בָּא בִּטְרוּנְיָא עִם בְּרִיּוֹתָיו),
וְכַאֲשֶׁר יִתְבּוֹנֵן תָּמִיד בָּזֶה יִהְיֶה לוֹ בְּוַדַּאי לְתוֹעֶלֶת
גְּדוֹלָה לְהִנָּצֵל מֵעָוֹן זֶה.

עוֹד יִמָּצֵא תּוֹעֶלֶת גְּדוֹלָה מִלִּמּוּד עִנְיָנִים אֵלּוּ,
שֶׁעַל-יְדֵי זֶה לֹא יִהְיֶה דָּבָר זֶה בְּעֵינָיו כְּהֶפְקֵר,
וְאָז אֲפִלּוּ אִם יִהְיֶה, חַס וְשָׁלוֹם, נִכְשָׁל בָּזֶה

will not be in the category of *baalei loshon hora*.[a] The Sages say in *Erachin* [15b] that being a *baal loshon hora* is equivalent to the three most severe sins [idolatry, adultery and murder], and that [the transgressor] will never greet the Divine Presence, and [is liable to other,] similarly severe punishments.[b] This is proven by the words of Rabbeinu Yonah in *Shaarei Teshuvah*[c] and by the words of *Kesef Mishneh*[d] to *Rambam, Hilchos De'os*, chapter seven. [On the other hand if one only occasionally speaks *loshon hora* it is not considered equivalent to the three most severe sins, but] only like any other negative precept.

[The benefit of being aware that one has sinned]

In addition, through this [study, if one does speak *loshon hora*] he will know in his soul that he has sinned before Hashem. [If a person does not even admit to himself

Yad Dovid

a. **baalei loshon hora:** These are people who continually and habitually speak *loshon hora*. For further discussion of this term see below, *Hilchos Loshon Hora*, ch. 1, *Be'er Mayim Chaim*, clause 6.

b. **similarly severe punishments:** See *Hilchos Loshon Hora*, ch. 1, *Mekor HaChaim*, clause 3.

לִפְרָקִים אֵינֶנּוּ בִּכְלַל בַּעֲלֵי לָשׁוֹן הָרָע - שֶׁעַל זֶה

אָמְרוּ חַז"ל בְּעֶרְכִין שֶׁשָּׁקוּל כְּנֶגֶד שְׁלֹשָׁה עֲוֹנוֹת

הַחֲמוּרוֹת וְאֵינָם מְקַבְּלִין פְּנֵי שְׁכִינָה וְכַיוֹצֵא

מֵעֳנָשִׁין הַחֲמוּרִין, כְּמוֹ שֶׁמּוּכָח מִדִּבְרֵי רַבֵּנוּ יוֹנָה

בְּ"שַׁעֲרֵי-תְשׁוּבָה"   וּמִדִּבְרֵי   הַ"כֶּסֶף-מִשְׁנֶה"

בְּרַמְבַּ"ם בְּפֶרֶק ז' מֵהִלְכוֹת דֵּעוֹת - רַק כִּשְׁאָר

לָאו דְּעָלְמָא.

גַּם עַל יְדֵי זֶה יֵדַע בְּנַפְשׁוֹ שֶׁחָטָא לִפְנֵי ה', וּכְמוֹ

Yad Dovid

c. **in Shaarei Teshuvah:** In *shaar* 3, clause 203 Rabbeinu Yonah says that this statement of the Sages applies to *baalei loshon hora.*

d. **Kesef Mishneh:** In *halachah* 1 there *Kesef Mishneh* explains that a person is termed a *baal loshon hora* only if he speaks *loshon hora* habitually, not just occasionally.

that he has done wrong, this provokes the judgment of Hashem,] as it is said (*Yirmiyahu* 2:35): "

"Behold, I shall enter into judgment against you because you said: 'I did not sin.' " [Moreover, if he knows he has transgressed] he will take measures to appease his fellow for this, or at least will make an effort not to speak [*loshon hora*] about him again. However this will not be the case if, heaven forbid, he ignores this subject and does not consider it a sin at all.[a]

I have also included in this work a long and comprehensive Introduction, in which I explain how many negative and positive precepts are commonly violated by someone who is not careful about this bitter sin of *loshon hora* and *rechilus*. (We find a similar device in the Mishnah in *Nedarim* 65b[b] and in *Menachos* 44a.[c] Perhaps Hashem will grant that the evil inclination will receive a blow when a person sees the tremendous destruction and ruin he makes through his speech.

[Studying the words of the Sages removes the evil inclination.]
In addition, besides these [benefits from the study of this subject], we know what *Midrash Rabbah* says in *Parashas Naso*

Yad Dovid

a. **at all:** This is the end of the note which began above, p.88.

b. *Nedarim* **65b:** There the Mishnah lists the various negative and positive precepts one violates by making certain vows.

שֶׁאָמַר הַכָּתוּב (ירמיה ב, לה): הִנְנִי נִשְׁפָּט אוֹתָךְ

עַל אָמְרֵךְ לֹא חָטָאתִי, וְיִרְאֶה לְפַיֵּס אֶת חֲבֵרוֹ עֲבוּר

זֶה אוֹ לְפָחוֹת שֶׁלֹּא לְדַבֵּר עָלָיו עוֹד הַפַּעַם, מַה

שֶּׁאֵין כֵּן אִם יַשְׁלִיךְ, חַס וְשָׁלוֹם, אֶת הַדָּבָר אַחַר

גֵּווֹ וְאֵינוֹ חוֹשְׁבוֹ לְעָוֹן כְּלָל.

גַּם חִבַּרְתִּי אֶל הַסֵּפֶר הַזֶּה פְּתִיחָה אֲרֻכָּה וּרְחָבָה, שָׁם מְבֹאָר כַּמָּה

לָאוִין וַעֲשִׂיִּין רָגִיל לַעֲבֹר מִי שֶׁאֵינוֹ נִזְהָר מֵאִסּוּר הַמַּר שֶׁל לָשׁוֹן הָרָע

וּרְכִילוּת [וּכְהַאי גַּוְנָא מָצִינוּ בְּמִשְׁנָה נְדָרִים (דַּף סה:), עַיֵּן שָׁם,

וּבִמְנָחוֹת (דַּף מד.), עַיֵּן שָׁם] – אוּלַי יִתֵּן ה' שֶׁעַל-יְדֵי כָּךְ יִנָּגֵף הַיֵּצֶר

בִּרְאוֹתוֹ אֶת גֹּדֶל הַמְּהוּמָה וְהַמַּכְשֵׁלָה שֶׁהוּא עוֹשֶׂה עַל-יְדֵי דִּבּוּרוֹ.

גַּם לְבַד זֶה, יָדוּעַ הוּא מַה שֶּׁהוּבָא בְּמִדְרַשׁ רַבָּה פָּרָשַׁת נָשֹׂא, וְזֶה

Yad Dovid

c. **Menachos 44a:** In the Gemara there Rav Sheshes lists the number of
precepts one violates by failing to observe certain mitzvos.

[14:4]: "If you toil diligently hard over the words [of the Sages], the Holy One, Blessed is He, removes the evil inclination from you." Therefore I said in my heart: 'Perhaps if people study this work, in which are gathered all the words of the *Rishonim* on this subject [of *loshon hora*], and if they contemplate it, the evil inclination will not have so much power over this sin.' When one withdraws oneself a little from this sin, it follows as a matter of course that as time goes on he will remove his hand from it altogether; for habit plays a large role in this sin, and "when one sets out to become pure [of sin], he is helped [by heaven]" (*Yoma* 38b). Through this merit, "A Redeemer will come to Zion" speedily, in our days, Amen.

לְשׁוֹנוֹ: אִם יָגַעְתָּ הַרְבֵּה בְּדִבְרֵיהֶם, הַקָדוֹשׁ-בָּרוּךְ- הוּא מֵסִיר יֵצֶר הָרָע מִמְּךָ. עַל-כֵּן אָמַרְתִּי אֶל לִבִּי: אֶפְשָׁר שֶׁעַל-יְדֵי שֶׁיְּעַיְּנוּ בְּסֵפֶר הַזֶּה, שֶׁהוּא מְלֻקָּט מִכָּל דִּבְרֵי הָרִאשׁוֹנִים בְּעִנְיָן זֶה, וְיִתְבּוֹנְנוּ בּוֹ, לֹא יִשְׁלֹט כָּל-כַּךְ הַיֵּצֶר הָרָע בְּעָוֹן זֶה; וּמִמֵּילָא כְּשֶׁיִּמְשֹׁךְ מִתְּחִלָּה אֶת עַצְמוֹ מֵעָוֹן זֶה בְּמִקְצָת, בְּהֶמְשֵׁךְ הַזְּמַן יִמְשֹׁךְ אֶת יָדוֹ מִמֶּנּוּ לְגַמְרֵי, כִּי בְּעָוֹן זֶה הַרְבֵּה מִמֶּנּוּ הַהֶרְגֵּל עוֹשֶׂה, וְהַבָּא לְטַהֵר מְסַיְּעִין אוֹתוֹ. וּבִזְכוּת זֶה – וּבָא לְצִיּוֹן גּוֹאֵל בִּמְהֵרָה בְּיָמֵינוּ, אָמֵן.

מקור החיים

כלל א׳

MEKOR HACHAIM

Chapter One

With

Be'er Mayim Chaim (precis)

Note: A superscript letter — e.g. ᵃ — in the text of *Mekor HaChaim* or *Be'er Mayim Chaim* refers to a comment in *Yad Dovid*; a superscript parenthetical number — e.g. (1) in the text of *Mekor HaChaim* refers to *Be'er Mayim Chaim*.

Each clause of *Mekor HaChaim* is followed by a precis (shortened version) of the relevant clauses of *Be'er Mayim Chaim*. The full version of *Be'er Mayim Chaim* will be found at the end of this book.

In *Mekor HaChaim* and *Be'er Mayim Chaim* square brackets are the translator's additions, while parentheses are those of *Chofetz Chaim*.

In the Hebrew text, a superscript letter refers to *Be'er Mayim Chaim*. For example, (א) refers to *Be'er Mayim Chaim*, clause 1.

THE PROHIBITIONS OF LOSHON HORA

Chapter One

This chapter will explain the prohibition against conveying *loshon hora* whether by direct speech, by hint, or by writing; the great punishment for one who makes a habit of this sin; and the reward for one who guards himself from this bitter sin; other details of the prohibition will also be discussed. The chapter contains nine clauses.

הִלְכוֹת אִיסּוּרֵי לָשׁוֹן הָרָע

כלל א׳

בִּכְלָל זֶה יְבוֹאָר אִיסּוּר סִיפּוּר לָשׁוֹן הָרַע בְּפִיו אוֹ עַל- יְדֵי רֶמֶז אוֹ מִכְתָּב, וְגוֹדֶל הָעוֹנֶשׁ לְמִי שֶׁהוּרְגָּל בַּעֲוֹן זֶה וְשָׂכָר לְמִי שֶׁשׁוֹמֵר עַצְמוֹ מֵעֲוֹן הַמַר הַזֶה, וְשְׁאָר הַפְּרָטִים, וּבוֹ ט׳ סְעִיפִים.

1. It is forbidden[a] to speak disparagingly about a Jew[b] even if the information related is completely[c] true;[1] and *Chazal* consistently refer to this as *loshon hora* [literally, "evil speech"].[d] (For if one's report contains an admixture of untruth[2] which increases the

Yad Dovid

a. forbidden: ...unless certain conditions are fulfilled, as detailed below, ch. 10, clause 2.

b. about a Jew: The prohibition refers specifically to *loshon hora* about a Jew, as is clear below, beginning of clause 6, where *Chofetz Chaim* adds the word יִשְׂרָאֵל ("a Jew"). Concerning whether there is a prohibition against speaking *loshon hora* about a non–Jew there is a dispute among the later authorities based upon *Midrash Rabbah, Devorim, Parashas Seitze* 9. *Radal* understands that there is a prohibition to speak *loshon hora* about a non-Jew. *Maharzu* understands that although there is no prohibition, nevertheless one should avoid speaking *loshon hora* about a non-Jew lest one become accustomed to speaking *loshon hora* and thereby come to speak *loshon hora* about a Jew. The majority of today's commentators interpret the *Midrash* in agreement with *Maharzu*. See *Tziunim Vehe'aros* 83 to *Sefer Orchos Chaim* with commentary of Rav Sarna; *Marpeh Loshon* pamphlet no. 7, p. 92; *Nesivos Chaim, Zera Chaim*, p. 392; *Ohev Yamim*, ch. 5, clause 4.

c. completely true: This phrase requires clarification. Rav Elchanan Wasserman, זצ"ל explains that, according to *Chofetz Chaim*, if we see someone commit a transgression there are two reasons why we are forbidden to relate this to others: (a) Perhaps the perpetrator does not know the seriousness of the prohibition he violated; for example, he may not know that it is a Scriptural prohibition; (b) Even if he understood the seriousness of the prohibition, perhaps his evil inclination overpowered him at the time, and now he regrets it. It follows that if it is clear to us that he knew the seriousness of the prohibition, and his evil inclination did not overpower him, and he has not regretted it, then we are permitted to tell others about it (*Kovetz Maamarim, Haflagah Leshevach Chavero*, p. 50, based on *Be'er Mayim Chaim* below, ch. 4, clause 33).However, this permission applies only if our intent is a constructive one, e.g., if publicizing the offense will help distance others from the path of the wicked, or might even bring the transgressor himself to repentance (see *Be'er Mayim Chaim* ch. 4, clause 32, condition "d"). The permission depends on other condi-

א. אָסוּר לְסַפֵּר בִּגְנוּת חֲבֵירוֹ אֲפִילוּ עַל אֱמֶת גָּמוּר⁽ᵃ⁾, וְזֶה נִקְרָא בְּפִי
חֲכָמֵינוּ זִכְרוֹנָם לִבְרָכָה בְּכָל מָקוֹם: לָשׁוֹן הָרַע, (דְּאִם יֵשׁ בְּהַסִּפּוּר
שֶׁלּוֹ תַּעֲרוֹבוֹת⁽ᵇ⁾ שֶׁל שֶׁקֶר וַעֲבוּר זֶה נִתְגַּנֶּה חֲבֵרוֹ יוֹתֵר הוּא

Yad Dovid

tions as well (ibid.).

Thus when *Chofetz Chaim* says here that it is forbidden to speak disparagingly about a Jew even if the information related is "completely true," he means that the objective fact is true; for example, that the person committed the transgression. This in itself does not make it permissible for us to relate it, since the subjective factors in the mind of the transgressor – unawareness of the seriousness of the prohibition, regret, and so on – may be such that the objective facts are misleading. On the other hand, when the entire account – even its derogatory implications about the subjective state of the transgressor – is "completely true," we are permitted to relate it, if all the necessary conditions are fulfilled (*Kovetz Ma'amarim*, loc. cit).

d. "evil speech:" Even if the listener does not believe the *loshon hora*, it is still forbidden to speak it. The very act of speaking with intent to disparage is enough to make the utterance forbidden, even with the permission of the person spoken about (below, ch. 3, *Mekor HaChaim* clause 6; and see Overview, para. 20, ch. 2, Be'er Mayim Chaim clause 28.). Even if the report contains no disparagement, it is forbidden if it could cause financial

Be'er Mayim Chaim - (Precis)

(1) Even if the information related is completely true: Chofetz Chaim cites three Talmud passages from which it may be deduced that loshon hora is forbidden even if the disparaging or damaging information is entirely true. He then cites three Rishonim — Rambam, Sefer Mitzvos Gadol, and Rabbeinu Yonah — who state this ruling explicitly; as well as two others — Rashi and Ramban — who imply it in their commentaries on the Chumash.

(2) An admixture of untruth: Chofetz Chaim cites a passage from Tractate Shevuos to prove that if a disparaging report contains even one word of untruth it constitutes the sin of motzi shem ra, false slander.

For the full version of each of the above Be'er Mayim Chaim, see below, p.132,136

113

disparagement,[a] this comes under the category of *motzi shem ra,* false slander,[b] and one's sin is far greater [than *loshon hora*]).[c] One who speaks *loshon hora* transgresses a negative precept, as it is said: "You shall not go about as a talebearer among your people"[(3)] [*Vayikra* 19:16]; and this[(4)] [verse prohibits *loshon hora,* since *loshon hora*] is included in [this prohibition of] *rechilus.*[d]

2. This negative precept is the one by which the Torah explicitly prohibits *loshon hora* and *rechilus.* But, as explained in the Introduction, in addition to this there are many other negative and positive precepts that a person transgresses if he speaks *loshon hora.*

3. All the above applies even if one only occasionally happens to speak disparagingly about his fellow Jew. But if, Heaven forbid, one is in the habit of constantly committing this sin, like

Yad Dovid

or bodily damage, distress or alarm to the person spoken about (see overview Sect. 8). However, in the latter case, if the person spoken about gave permission, the report is permitted. (below Ch. 2 *Be'er Mayim Chaim* clause 28).

a. **which increases the disparagement:** I.e., his good name will be damaged even more.

b. **false slander:** Moreover, even if one does not actually lie, but merely exaggerates the disparagement, it is also considered *motzi shem ra* (*Hilchos Loshon Hora,* ch. 5, clause 2). Only in certain cases is one permitted to exaggerate (see *Hilchos Loshon Hora,* ch. 4, *Be'er Mayim Chaim,* clause 43).

c. **one's sin is far greater [than loshon hora]:** This is because *motzi shem ra* is a lie (*Be'er Mayim Chaim* below, clause 3). According to *Rabbeinu Yonah, Shaarei Teshuvah* 3:55, *motzi shem ra* carries the penalty of death by the hand of heaven.

114

בִּכְלַל מוֹצִיא שֵׁם רַע, וַעֲוֹנוֹ גָּדוֹל הַרְבֵּה יוֹתֵר.) וְהַמְסַפֵּר עוֹבֵר בְּלֹא

תַעֲשֶׂה, שֶׁנֶּאֱמַר: (וִיקְרָא יט,ט"ז) לֹא תֵלֵךְ רָכִיל בְּעַמֶּךָ ^(ג), וְזֶה ^(ד)

גַּם-כֵּן בִּכְלַל רְכִילוּת הוּא.

ב. הַלָּאו הַזֶּה שֶׁכָּתַבְנוּ, הוּא מַה שֶּׁכָּתַבְתּוּ הַתּוֹרָה בְּפֵרוּשׁ מְיֻחָד

לְאִסּוּר זֶה שֶׁל לָשׁוֹן הָרָע וּרְכִילוּת, אֲבָל כְּלָאו הָכֵי יֵשׁ עוֹד הַרְבֵּה

לָאוִין וַעֲשִׂיִּין אֲחֵרִים שֶׁהוּא עוֹבֵר עֲלֵיהֶן עַל-יְדֵי סִפּוּר הָרָע הַזֶּה,

כַּמְבֹאָר לְעֵיל בַּפְּתִיחָה הַקּוֹדֶמֶת, עַיֵּן שָׁם.

ג. כָּל זֶה – אֲפִילוּ אִם רַק בְּמִקְרֶה סִפֵּר גְּנוּת חֲבֵרוֹ, אֲבָל אִם, חַס

וְשָׁלוֹם, הֻרְגַּל בְּעָוֹן זֶה בִּתְמִידוּת, כְּמוֹ אֵלּוּ שֶׁרְגִילִין תָּמִיד ^(ה)

Yad Dovid

d. included in [this prohibition of] rechilus: *Loshon hora* itself does not necessarily incite hatred. Thus, for the explanation of how *loshon hora* is included in *rechilus* see *Be'er Mayim Chaim* below, clause 4.

Be'er Mayim Chaim - (Precis)

(3) You shall not go about as a talebearer among your people: Chofetz Chaim cites *Rambam* and *Sefer Mitzvos Gadol*, who state that this verse refers to *loshon hora* and *rechilus*.

(4) And this [verse prohibits loshon hora, since loshon hora is included in this prohibition of rechilus]: Rambam *maintains that our verse refers to* rechilus, *and from this one may deduce by* kal vechomer *(a fortiori) that* loshon hora *is forbidden, since* loshon hora *is worse than* rechilus. Ravad, *on the other hand, maintains that* rechilus *is worse than* loshon hora *and therefore the prohibition of* loshon hora *cannot be deduced by* kal vechomer *from our verse.* Chofetz Chaim *discusses other possible Scriptural sources from which* Ravad *(and other Rishonim) might derive the prohibition against* loshon hora.

For the full version of each of the above Be'er Mayim Chaim, see below, p.136, 140

those[5] who are accustomed always to sit and say: 'This is how so-and-so acts; this is how his ancestors acted; this is what I heard about him...' and these are disparaging remarks – people like these are referred to by the Sages as "habitual slanderers" (*baalei loshon hora*),[a] and their punishment is far worse,[b] since they brazenly and maliciously transgress *Hashem*'s Torah and they act as if this prohibition did not exist, as explained at the end of the Introduction.[c] About them the verse says: "May *Hashem* cut off [d] all flattering lips, the tongue that speaks grandly (*gedolos*)"[e] (*Tehillim* 12:4).

Yad Dovid

a. baalei loshon hora: Literally, "owners" or "masters" of *loshon hora*, those for whom speaking *loshon hora* is an integral part of their lifestyle.

b. their punishment is far worse: It is far worse than the punishment of those who only occasionally speak *loshon hora*, for *baalei loshon hora* have no share in the world to come, as explained below, *Mekor HaChaim*, clause 4.

It should be noted, however, that even if one only occasionally speaks *loshon hora* he is liable to the punishment of *tzaraas* ("leprosy") if his words cause the listener to believe the *loshon hora* and relate it to others (see below, ch. 3, *Be'er Mayim Chaim*, clause 6; for the implications of "leprosy" in our time, see Overview, note 35). Also, one may lose part of his merits, because they are transferred to the person about whom he spoke the *loshon hora* while that person's transgressions are transferred to one's own account. (See *Chovos Halevavos, Shaar Ha'anavah*, ch. 7.) The amount of merits and sins transferred is according to the intent and weight of the *loshon hora* spoken. A relatively minor utterance of *loshon hora* transfers a small amount; a more damaging utterance transfers more. The *Maggid Mesharim* affirms the reality of this "transfer of accounts" mentioned by

לֵישֵׁב וּלְסַפֵּר: כָּךְ וְכָךְ עָשָׂה פְלוֹנִי, כָּךְ וְכָךְ עָשׂוּ אֲבוֹתָיו, כָּךְ וְכָךְ
שָׁמַעְתִּי עָלָיו, וְהוּא דְבָרִים שֶׁל גְּנוּת – אֲנָשִׁים כָּאֵלוּ הֵם נִקְרָאִין בְּפִי
חַז"ל בְּשֵׁם בַּעֲלֵי לָשׁוֹן הָרָע, וְעָנְשָׁן הַרְבֵּה יוֹתֵר גָּדוֹל, אַחֲרֵי
שֶׁבִּשְׁאָט נַפְשָׁם וּזְדוֹן לִבָּם עוֹבְרִין עַל תּוֹרַת ה' וְנַעֲשָׂה זֶה אֶצְלָם
כְּהֶפְקֵר, כְּמוֹ שֶׁמְּבֹאָר לְעֵיל בְּסוֹף הַפְּתִיחָה, וַעֲלֵיהֶם נֶאֱמַר בְּקַבָּלָה:
יַכְרֵת ה' כָּל שִׂפְתֵי חֲלָקוֹת לָשׁוֹן מְדַבֶּרֶת גְּדֹלוֹת (תהלים יב,ד).

Yad Dovid

Chovos Halevavos. This is a matter of "measure for measure" (מִדָּה כְּנֶגֶד מִדָּה):
To the extent that the speaker wants to degrade and detract from the merits of the one spoken about — to that same extent are his own merits detracted from him by heaven (*Hamarpeh Lenefesh,* quoted by *Marpeh Loshon,* pamphlet 5, p.79).

c. at the end of the Introduction: In "Curses," beginning of clause 3.

d. cut off: This alludes to the loss of a share in the world to come (*Radal* to *Pirkei DeRabbi Eliezer,* ch. 53, clause 2).

e. gedolos. The Jerusalem *Talmud* (*Pe'ah* 1:1; p. 4a) explains that *gedolos* alludes to *loshon hora* because (as mentioned below, *Mekor HaChaim,* clause 4) the sin of *loshon hora* is equivalent to the sins of idolatry, forbidden relations and murder. The *Gemara* there cites a verse for each of these sins to show that the transgressor is punished in this world but the main punishment is reserved for him in the world to come; and in each of those verses we find the expression *gadol* (sing. of *gedolos*); therefore our verse uses the plural form, *gedolos,* since it deals with *loshon hora,* which includes these three other sins (*Pnei Moshe* to the Jerusalem *Talmud* there). But in what case is *loshon hora* considered equivalent to these three sins? In the case of "habitual slanderers," *baalei loshon hora* (*Mekor HaChaim* below, clause 4). Thus it is clear that the punishment for such people is as the

Be'er Mayim Chaim - (Precis)

(5) Like those who are accustomed always to sit and say: *Chofetz Chaim gives the explicit source in Rambam.*

For the full version of this Be'er Mayim Chaim, see below, p.150

4. *Chazal* say:[6] There are three sins for which a person is punished in this world and has no share in the world to come. These
are: idolatry, forbidden relations, and murder; and *loshon hora* is
equivalent to all of them. *Chazal* quote verses to prove this. The
Rishonim explain that it refers to those who are habituated to
commit this sin constantly,ᵃ and who do not agree to guard themselves from it, because in their mind it is like something
permitted.

5. Regarding the prohibition against relating *loshon hora*, it
makes no difference whether one spoke on his own initiative
because he wanted to, or whether someone else was insistent
with him,[7] talking and pleading with him until he related the
facts; in either case it is forbidden. Even with his father or his
rebbe,[8] whom he is obligated to honor and revere, and not to

Yad Dovid

verse says here, "May Hashem cut off..." this being a worse punishment
than for those who only occasionally speak *loshon hora*. In other words, as
explained in *Be'er Mayim Chaim* here, the person who is a *baal loshon hora*,
if he does not repent of his *loshon hora*, loses his share in the world to
come. Also the Divine Presence does not rest upon him, as mentioned
above, *Be'er Mayim Chaim*, clause 1.

a. **habituated to commit this sin constantly:** I.e., they are *baalei loshon hora*
(see above, *Mekor HaChaim*, clause 3).
We find that the *Gemara* in *Sanhedrin* 74a brings a verse for each one of
these three sins, to show that one must give up his life rather than transgress them (see *Yoreh De'ah* 157:1 for details of this *halachah*). If *loshon hora*
is equivalent to all of them, is one then required to give up his life rather
than be a *baal loshon hora*? It is clear from *Mekor HaChaim*, clause 6 that
Chofetz Chaim understands that this is not required, since he says that one
is required to give up all his money and not transgress the prohibition of
loshon hora (*Marpeh Loshon*,pamphlet 3, p. 45). Thus one is only

ד. אָמְרוּ [ו] חַז"ל: עַל שָׁלֹשׁ עֲבֵרוֹת נִפְרָעִין מִן הָאָדָם בָּעוֹלָם הַזֶּה וְאֵין לוֹ חֵלֶק לָעוֹלָם הַבָּא, וְאֵלּוּ הֵן: עֲבוֹדָה-זָרָה וְגִלּוּי עֲרָיוֹת וּשְׁפִיכוּת דָּמִים, וְלָשׁוֹן הָרָע נֶגֶד כֻּלָּן. וְהֵבִיאוּ חַז"ל עַל זֶה רְאָיָה מִן הַכְּתוּבִים. וּפֵרְשׁוּ הָרִאשׁוֹנִים דְּהַכַּוָּנָה עַל אֵלּוּ שֶׁהֻרְגְּלוּ בְּעָוֹן זֶה בִּתְמִידוּת וְאֵין מְקַבְּלִים עַל עַצְמָם לְהִשָּׁמֵר מִמֶּנּוּ מִפְּנֵי שֶׁנַּעֲשָׂה הַדָּבָר אֶצְלָם כְּהֶתֵּר.

ה. אֵין חִלּוּק בְּאִסּוּר הַסִּפּוּר, בֵּין אִם סִפֵּר מֵעַצְמוֹ בִּרְצוֹנוֹ וּבֵין אִם עָמַד עָלָיו [ז] חֲבֵרוֹ בִּדְבָרִים וְהִפְצִירוֹ עַד שֶׁיְּסַפֵּר לוֹ, מִכָּל מָקוֹם אָסוּר. וַאֲפִילוּ אָבִיו אוֹ רַבּוֹ [ח] שֶׁמְּחֻיָּב בִּכְבוֹדָם וּבְמוֹרָאָם שֶׁלֹּא

Yad Dovid

obligated to give up his money, but not his life. *Rabbeinu Yonah* in *Shaarei Teshuvah* 3:202 - 210 discusses how it is possible that *loshon hora* can be equivalent to such sins which one is required to give up his life rather than transgress.

Be'er Mayim Chaim - (Precis)

(6) Chazal say: *Chofetz Chaim discusses whether one who habitually speaks loshon hora has no share in the world to come, or is simply punished there. He concludes that such a person has no share in the world to come.*

(7) Insistent with him: *This law is derived from the story of Do'eg and King Shaul. Do'eg is considered guilty of having spoken rechilus about Dovid, even though he did so at the insistence of King Shaul. The same principle applies to loshon hora.*

(8) His father or his rebbe: *If one sees his father or rebbe committing a transgression, one must reprove him, despite the fact that one is obligated to honor him. All the more so, if one's father or rebbe instructs one to commit a transgression, one must refuse.*

This can also be proven from the Gemara in Shevuos [31a] which states that if one's rebbe asks him to become involved in even a hint of a falsehood, one is forbidden to do so.

Another proof is found in Sanhedrin [49a], where the Gemara says that if a king of Israel commands one to transgress a Torah prohibition, one must not do so. All the more so, one must not obey the command of one's father or rebbe to speak loshon hora.

For the full version of each of the above Be'er Mayim Chaim, see below, p.150,152,154

contradict their words, if they ask him[9] to tell them about a certain matter, and he knows that within the report he will inevitably come to speak *loshon hora* or even just *avak loshon hora*[a], he
is forbidden to comply with their request.[b]

6. Even if one sees that if he accustoms himself to this trait of
never speaking disparagingly about a Jew and never uttering
other types of forbidden speech, it will cause him a major loss of
livelihood; for example where he is employed by others, and
they are people who do not have the aroma of Torah learning;
and as is known, due to our manifold iniquities people of this
sort are very licentious in this severe sin, even to the extent that
if they see someone who is not as loose-tongued as they are, they
consider him a fool and a simpleton, and due to this they will
dismiss him from his job, and he will have no income to support

Yad Dovid

a. *avak loshon hora*: See Overview, para. 22.

b. **forbidden to comply with their request**: However, if they specify that
it is for a constructive purpose (תועלת), then it appears that one may rely
on this and relate the information to them, even though one cannot see the
constructive purpose in it. However, if one perceives that the inquirer is
not knowledgeable about the definition of "constructive purpose," then
certainly the *halachah* changes (*Nesivos Chaim, Nesiv Chaim,* clause 7; *Chelkas Binyomin, sif katan* 8). The problem in such a case is how to avoid telling them the *loshon hora,* for if one says: 'It is forbidden for me to speak
loshon hora,' this in itself is *avak loshon hora.* On the other hand, simply to

לִסְתֹּר דִּבְרֵיהֶם, אִם הֵם בִּקְשׁוּ מִמֶּנּוּ[ט] שֶׁיְסַפֵּר לָהֶם עִנְיָן פְּלוֹנִי
וּפְלוֹנִי, וְהוּא יוֹדֵעַ שֶׁבְּתוֹךְ הַסִּפּוּר יִכְרַח לָבוֹא לִידֵי לָשׁוֹן הָרָע אוֹ
אֲפִילוּ רַק לְאָבָק שֶׁל לָשׁוֹן הָרָע, אָסוּר לוֹ לְשַׁמֵּעַ לָהֶם.

ו. אֲפִילוּ אִם הוּא רוֹאֶה, שֶׁאִם יַרְגִּיל עַצְמוֹ בַּמִּדָּה הַזֹּאת שֶׁלֹּא לְסַפֵּר
לְעוֹלָם בִּגְנוּתוֹ שֶׁל יִשְׂרָאֵל וְכַדּוֹמֶה מִדְּבוּרִים הָאֲסוּרִים, יְסַבֵּב לוֹ
הֶפְסֵד גָּדוֹל בְּעִנְיַן פַּרְנָסָתוֹ, כְּגוֹן שֶׁהוּא תַּחַת רְשׁוּת אֲחֵרִים, וְהֵם
אֲנָשִׁים שֶׁאֵין בָּהֶם רֵיחַ תּוֹרָה, וְיָדוּעַ הוּא שֶׁבַּעֲווֹנוֹתֵינוּ הָרַבִּים
אֲנָשִׁים כָּאֵלּוּ הֵם פְּרוּצִים מְאֹד בְּזֶה הֶעָוֹן הֶחָמוּר, עַד שֶׁאִם יִרְאוּ מִי
שֶׁאֵין פִּיו פָּתוּחַ כָּל-כָּךְ כְּמוֹתָם יַחֲזִיקוּ אוֹתוֹ לְשׁוֹטֶה וָפֶתִי,
וְעַל-יְדֵי זֶה יְסַלְּקוּהוּ מִמִּשְׂמַרְתּוֹ וְלֹא יִהְיֶה לוֹ בַּמֶּה לְפַרְנֵס אֶת
בְּנֵי-בֵיתוֹ,

Yad Dovid

the request would be disrespectful towards one's parent. What, then, is to
be done? We clearly see below (*Hilchos Loshon Hora*, ch. 4, *Be'er Mayim
Chaim* clause 48 s.v. "ויותר טוב") that one may lie about a situation in order
to avoid speaking *loshon hora* (see *Titen Emes LeYaakov*, by HaRav Hagaon
R' Yaakov Fish, ch. 2, clause 24). Therefore this would certainly be a
counsel in the present case, if the lie would be plausible to the parent.
(For a discussion of a teacher who asks pupils in a class to reveal which
pupil did a certain bad action, see *Igros Moshe, Yoreh De'ah*, vol. 2, *siman*
103. And see *Chelkas Binyomin*, loc. cit. for further discussion.)

Be'er Mayim Chaim - (Precis)

(9) If they ask him: *Chofetz Chaim explains why he did not mention the simplest case, namely where one's father or rebbe asks one to speak loshon hora
itself.*

*He also explains that even if they were to ask one to commit a sin, this would not
remove them from the class of "Your People." Thus one would still be obligated
to honor them — but not to the extent of committing a sin at their command.*

For the full version of this Be'er Mayim Chaim, see below, p.158

his family — nevertheless even in these circumstances one is forbidden to speak *loshon hora*ᵃ, just as with all other negative precepts,[10] concerning which one is obligated to give up everything he owns rather than transgress one of them, as is explained in *Yoreh De'ah* (157:1, in *Hagoh*).

7. And from this[b] we can discern that, all the more so, if it is only one's honor that is at stake[c] — for example, he is sitting with a group of people and there is no way to slip away from them, and they are speaking things that are forbidden according to *Halachah*, and if he sits silently and does not add anything at all to their tales he will appear in their eyes like one who is mentally deranged — certainly[11] it is forbidden.[d] About this and similar situations *Chazal* said [*Eduyos* 5:6]: "It is better for a person to be called a fool his whole life, than to be wicked for

Yad Dovid

a. **nevertheless even in these circumstances one is forbidden to speak loshon hora:** If someone is personally trying to cause harm to us, and speaking *loshon hora* about him would serve the constructive purpose of preventing that harm, one is permitted to speak it. (See *Hilchos Loshon Hora*, ch. 10, for conditions of this permission.) However in our case there is no permission, since the person about whom the *loshon hora* is spoken is not trying to harm one's livelihood.

One is permitted to lie in order to avoid speaking *loshon hora* (see above page 121, *Yad Dovid, clause b*). If so, in the case mentioned here why should one give up his job? Why not just invent some lie in order to escape speaking *loshon hora*? The answer could be that it is a case where for some reason the lie would not be believed. *Ikrei Dinim (Hilchos Loshon*

עַל-פִּי כֵן אָסוּר, כְּכָל שְׁאָר לַאוִין[׳] שֶׁמְחֻיָּב לִתֵּן כָּל אֲשֶׁר לוֹ וְלֹא

לַעֲבֹר עֲלֵיהֶן, כַּמְבֹאָר בְּיוֹרֶה דֵעָה (סִימָן קנז, סְעִיף א, בַּהַגָּ"ה), עַיֵן שָׁם.

ז. וּמִזֶּה נוּכַל לֵידַע דְּכָל-שֶׁכֵּן אִם נוֹגֵעַ לוֹ רַק בִּכְבוֹד בְּעָלְמָא, כְּגוֹן

שֶׁיּוֹשֵׁב בֵּין חֲבוּרַת אֲנָשִׁים וְאֵין לוֹ עֵצָה אֵיךְ לְהִשָּׁמֵט מֵהֶם, וְהֵם אַף

מְדַבְּרִים בִּדְבָרִים הָאֲסוּרִים עַל-פִּי דִין, וּכְשֶׁיִּהְיֶה יוֹשֵׁב וְדוֹמֵם וְלֹא

יְסַיֵּעַ עִמָּם בְּסִפּוּרֵיהֶם כְּלָל יֵחָשֵׁב בְּעֵינֵיהֶם כְּמִשְׁתַּגֵּעַ, בְּוַדַּאי

דְּאָסוּר[׳א]. וְעַל זֶה וְכַיּוֹצֵא בָּזֶה אָמְרוּ חֲזַ"ל: (עדויות פ"ה מ"ו) מוּטָב

לָאָדָם שֶׁיִּקָּרֵא שׁוֹטֶה כָּל יָמָיו וְאַל יִהְיֶה רָשָׁע שָׁעָה אַחַת לִפְנֵי

הַמָּקוֹם. וִיזָרֵז עַצְמוֹ בִּשְׁעַת מַעֲשֶׂה בְּכָל כֹּחוֹתָיו לַעֲמֹד עַל נַפְשׁוֹ

Yad Dovid

Hora ch. 6, note 4) states that even if one's employment situation does not force him to speak *loshon hora*, but only to hear it, he must leave his job, since he is in danger of believing the *loshon hora* which he hears.

b. and from this: From what was said above, clause 6.

c. at stake: One's refraining from *loshon hora* will not cause him loss of income, but only loss of esteem.

d. forbidden: It is forbidden for him to speak *loshon hora* in order to avoid being considered a fool.

Be'er Mayim Chaim - (Precis)

(10) **Just as with all other negative precepts:** *Loshon hora is a very severe prohibition, because it commonly involves a number of other Torah violations. Thus if one must sacrifice all one's possessions to avoid other Scriptural prohibitions, then all the more so one must do so to avoid speaking loshon hora. In fact, however, one is not allowed to transgress even a Rabbinic prohibition in order to save one's possessions.*

(11) **Certainly it is forbidden:** *The precept of the Sages that one should be involved in social life does not apply in a case like this. Even if people will hate him for not taking part in their conversation, he must not fear this at all.*

For the full version of each of the above Be'er Mayim Chaim, see below, p.158,160

one moment before the Almighty." He should muster all his
strength to control himself at the moment of trial, and he can be
confident in his heart that he will receive infinite reward for
this from *Hashem*, Blessed be He. As *Chazal* say [*Avos* 5:23]:
"The reward [for a *mitzvah*] is in proportion to the suffering
[one endures in order to fulfill it]." And it is stated in *Avos
DeRabbi Nassan* [3:6]: "A hundred times[a] with suffering, more
than one without suffering." (The meaning is: When one must
suffer in order to do a *mitzvah* or refrain from a transgression,
his reward is a hundred times greater than when he does the
identical *mitzvah* without suffering.) And concerning a time like
this the dictum of *Chazal* in the *Midrash [Even Shleimah 7:1]* is
certainly applicable: "Every single moment that a person keeps
his mouth closed [from forbidden speech], he merits the Hidden
Light[b] which no angel or person can imagine." As for how one
should act if caught in an evil group like this, regarding the
duty to rebuke them [for their *loshon hora*] and the duty not to
believe what they say, see below [ch. 6, clauses 4-6]. And see
Introduction above, "Negative Precepts'" [clause 16], which is
relevant to this topic.

Yad Dovid

a. a hundred times: The text there reads: "One time with suffering, more
than a hundred times without suffering," i.e: "[The reward for doing a
mitzvah] one time with suffering [is] more than [for doing it] a hundred
times without suffering." But according to the version given here, one
must interpret: "[The reward is] a hundred times [more for doing one
mitzvah] with suffering... than [for doing a similar] one without suffering."

b. hidden Light: אוֹר הַגָּנוּז (*Or Haganuz*), the light of the first days of
Creation, which was hidden away for the righteous to enjoy in the world
to come.

וְיִהְיֶה נָכוֹן לִבּוֹ בָּטוּחַ כִּי שְׂכָרוֹ יִהְיֶה עֲבוּר זֶה מִן הַשֵּׁם יִתְבָּרַךְ עַד
אֵין קֵץ, כְּמַאֲמַר חֲזַ"ל: (אבות פ"ה מכ"ג) לְפֻם צַעֲרָא אַגְרָא.
וְאִיתָא בְּאָבוֹת דְּרַבִּי נָתָן (פ"ג מ"ו), כִּי מֵאָה פְּעָמִים בְּצַעַר מִפַּעַם
אֶחָד שֶׁלֹּא בְּצַעַר (וּבֵאוּרוֹ, כִי לַעֲשׂוֹת דָּבָר　מִצְוָה אוֹ לִפְרֹשׁ מִדָּבָר
אָסוּר שֶׁבָּא לוֹ עַל-יְדֵי צַעַר, שְׂכָרוֹ מֵאָה פְּעָמִים יוֹתֵר מִמִּצְוָה אַחֶרֶת
כְּמוֹתָהּ שֶׁבָּא לוֹ שֶׁלֹּא בְּצַעַר). וְעַל עֵת כָּזֶה בְּוַדַּאי שַׁיָּךְ מַאֲמַר חֲזַ"ל
בַּמִּדְרָשׁ: (ראה אבן שלמה פ"ז ה"א) כָּל רֶגַע וָרֶגַע שֶׁאָדָם חוֹסֵם
פִּיו זוֹכֶה לָאוֹר הַגָּנוּז שֶׁאֵין כָּל מַלְאָךְ וּבְרִיָּה יָכוֹל לְשַׁעֵר. וְלָעִנְיָן
אֵיךְ יִתְנַהֵג אִם נִתְפַּס בַּחֲבוּרָה רָעָה כָּזוֹ לְעִנְיַן הוֹכָחָה וְקַבָּלָה, עַיֵּן
לְקַמָּן בִּכְלָל ו' סָעִיפִים ד' ה' ו'. וְעַיֵּן לְעֵיל בַּפְּתִיחָה בְּלָאוִין (אוֹת
טז), כִּי שַׁיָּךְ לְכָאן.

125

8. This prohibition of loshon hora applies whether one actually speaks about him [the target of the *loshon hora* or writes[a] the matter about him.[12] Likewise it makes no difference whether one relates one's *loshon hora* about him explicitly or relates the *loshon hora* about him by way of bodily[b] gesture. [13] In all forms[14] it is in the category of *loshon hora.*[c]

Yad Dovid

a. writes: This means that without a definite constructive purpose it is forbidden to write *loshon hora* in newspapers. *Nesivos Chaim,* pp. 296-305 discusses this subject of *loshon hora* and *rechilus* in newspapers at great length. He deals with questions such as the following: What is the *halachah* regarding readers' believing *loshon hora* printed in a newspaper? Which subjects is one allowed to read? What type of *loshon hora* are journalists susceptible to stumble in, and to cause others to stumble? What forms of *avak loshon hora* appear in newspapers? Who transgresses the sin of *loshon hora* (the journalist, the printer, the editor, the typesetter, the administrator, etc.)? Note: The goal of providing exciting or interesting news is not considered a constructive purpose; rather, a constructive purpose is, for example, warning people about something which could harm them. Some further points: It is an error to think that if a newspaper has printed *loshon hora* it has become a "matter of public knowledge" (דָּבָר מְפוּרְסָם; see there; and see Overview, para. 23). Drawing a disparaging caricature of someone also falls under the prohibition of *loshon hora* (*Ohev Yamim,* ch. 3, clause 10).

ח. אָסוּר זֶה שֶׁל לָשׁוֹן הָרָע הוּא בֵּין אִם הוּא מְסַפֵּר עָלָיו בְּפִיו

מַמָּשׁ אוֹ שֶׁהוּא כּוֹתֵב עָלָיו[יב] דָּבָר זֶה בְּמִכְתָּבוֹ, וְגַם אֵין בּוֹ חִלּוּק

בֵּין אִם הוּא מְסַפֵּר עָלָיו הַלָּשׁוֹן הָרָע שֶׁלּוֹ בְּפֵרוּשׁ וּבֵין אִם הוּא

מְסַפֵּר עָלָיו הַלָּשׁוֹן הָרָע בְּדֶרֶךְ רֶמֶז[יג] — בְּכָל גַּוְנֵי[יד] בִּכְלַל לָשׁוֹן

הָרָע הוּא.

Yad Dovid

b. by way of bodily gesture: For example, saying that someone is very talented, while winking an eye to show that the opposite is meant. This should not be confused with *avak loshon hora*, which is a Rabbinic prohibition (as above, end of *Be'er Mayim Chaim*, clause 8, s.v. דאפילו לאבק לשון הרע). The difference is that in our present case the person indicates the derogatory information itself (albeit by gesture or facial expression rather than speech); hence this constitutes *loshon hora* on the Scriptural level. By contrast, in speaking *avak loshon hora* the person does not directly indicate the derogatory information, but only implies it, or says something which could lead others to speak *loshon hora* (see *Hilchos Loshon Hora*, ch. 9, *Be'er Mayim Chaim*, clause 2).

c. in the category of *loshon hora*: That is, it is a Scriptural prohibition.

Be'er Mayim Chaim - (Precis)

(12) Or writes the matter about him: Chofetz Chaim proves from Scripture that loshon hora communicated by writing is forbidden. He also cites the Gemara (Sanhedrin 30a) which is based on the premise that a court verdict delivered in writing should be phrased in such a way as to avoid rechilus.

(13) By way of bodily gesture: Chofetz Chaim cites Onkelos and Rashi to Parashas Kedoshim (Vayikra 19:16), as well as verses in Mishlei (6:12-13), to prove that gestures and hints can constitute loshon hora. He reconciles this with the Gemara (Berachos 8a) which permits a bridegroom to hint that his wife is bad; and with the Gemara (Yevamos 63b) where one of the Sages tells his son that his wife (the son's mother) fits the description: "more bitter than death."

(14) In all forms: Chofetz Chaim proves that it is possible to violate the prohibition against loshon hora simply by showing a letter that someone wrote.

For the full version of each of the above Be'er Mayim Chaim,
see below, p.160, 162, 164

9. Furthermore, know that even if within the disparagement with which he deprecates his fellow Jew he also attributes the self-same defect to himself, and even if he begins[15] by disparaging himself first[a] regarding this defect — even so it does not escape the category of *loshon hora.*[b]

Yad Dovid

a. disparaging himself first: Before speaking *loshon hora* about the other person he says the same thing about himself.

b. the category of *loshon hora:* Why does *Chofetz Chaim* need to inform us that this is considered *loshon hora?* Why would we think that just because one attributes the selfsame defect to himself it should not be considered *loshon hora* when one says it about his fellow Jew? *Nesivos Chaim* (*Nesiv Chaim*, clause 12) suggests that perhaps the intent of *Chofetz Chaim* is as follows: When a person states something bad about himself, presumably he does not mean it as disparagement, but only means to express his distress over his difficult situation (just as *Be'er Mayim Chaim* explains here regarding the Prophet Yeshayahu). If so, then one might think that what he says about his fellow Jew [in the case where he says it first about himself] is also merely an expression of distress and is not meant to disparage. To dispel this notion, *Chofetz Chaim* informs us that, nevertheless, it does not escape the category of *loshon hora.*

ט. וְדַע עוֹד, דַּאֲפִלוּ אִם בְּתוֹךְ הַגְּנוּת שֶׁגִּנָּה אֶת חֲבֵרוֹ גִּנָּה אֶת עַצְמוֹ

^(טו) גַּם-כֵּן בְּזֶה הַגְּנוּת גּוּפָא, וַאֲפִלוּ הִקְדִּים לְהִתְרָעֵם עַל עַצְמוֹ בָּזֶה,

אֲפִילוּ הָכֵי מִכְּלַל דֵּילָטוֹרְיָא לָא נַפְקֵי.

Be'er Mayim Chaim - (Precis)

(15) Even if he begins by disparaging himself first: *Chofetz Chaim proves this law from the verse in Yeshayahu (6:5) where the Prophet is punished for stating that both he and his People are "of contaminated lips."*

For the full version of this Be'er Mayim Chaim, see below, p.166

באר מים חיים

BE'ER MAYIM CHAIM

(full version)

to Chapter One of

Mekor HaChaim

The text of *Be'er Mayim Chaim*, which earlier was presented in the shortened form (precis) is here presented in full.

At the beginning of each *Be'er Mayim Chaim* the reader will find a reference to the place in *Mekor HaChaim* to which this *Be'er Mayim Chaim* refers: for example:

[to *Mekor HaChaim*, clause 1, p.112].

Then follows, in bold type, the relevant words in *Mekor HaChaim* to which *Be'er Mayim Chaim* refers, for example:

Even if the information related is completely true:

This is followed by the full translation of *Be'er Mayim Chaim*.

(1) [to *Mekor HaChaim* clause 1, p. 112]: **Even if the information related is completely true:** This is the first mistake people usually make: [They think that if the *loshon hora* is true, it must be permissible to relate it.] Therefore I shall bring three proofs from the Gemara, and afterwards from the halachic authorities, [to show] that the prohibition of *loshon hora* applies even if the information related is true. The first proof is as follows:

The Gemara in *Moed Katan* (16a) states that in the case of an emissary sent by the *beis din* to summon a litigant, if the litigant responds insultingly the emissary is permitted to relate this to the *beis din* and his report is not a transgression. *Rashi* explains that the case is where the litigant insulted the emissary, who then reported to the *beis din:* "He insulted me."

The Gemara derives this permission from a verse in *Parashas Korach* [where Moshe Rabbeinu sent an emissary to summon Dosan and Aviram, and they replied (*Bamidbar* 16:14):] "Will you put out the eyes of these men? [We will not go up!"].[a] [According to *Rashi's* interpretation of this Gemara, then] these insulting words were addressed to the emissary himself; presumably the emissary reported this to Moshe[b].

Thus the Gemara proves that the emissary is permitted to say [the derogatory information to the *beis din*]. Now, according to *Rashi's* interpretation, the Gemara is discussing a question of *loshon hora*[c], and the emissary himself knew that it was true that Dosan and Aviram had insulted him, since they said to him "Will you put out the eyes of those men?[d] [We will not go up!"]

Here we have a case where someone related true derogatory information; yet the Gemara explains that he was permitted to do so only because he was an emissary of the *beis din*.[e] Clearly, then, someone who is not an emissary of the *beis din* is forbidden to relate derogatory information even if it is true!

Yad Dovid

a. will you put out the eyes of these men, etc: This means, even if you were to send someone to put out our eyes if we would not come up to you, we still would not come up (*Rashi* to *Chumash*).

(א) אמת גמור. ולפי שזה הוא הטעות הראשון שרגילין העולם לטעות בו על כן
אביא לך על זה ג' עדים מן הגמרא ואחר כך מכל הפוסקים דאיסורו הוא אפילו
על אמת. וזה, דגרסינן במועד קטן (ט"ז ע"א) מנלן דאי מיתפקר בשלוחא דבי
דינא, ואתי ואמר, לא מיתחזי כלישנא בישא, דכתיב העיני האנשים ההם תנקר,
ועיין בפירוש רש"י בד"ה דאי מיתפקר, שפירש שחירף שליח בית דין ושליח
אמר חרפני, ועל זה מייתי הגמרא ראיה מקרא העיני וכו' ואשליח קאי, ומסתמא
אמר לו השליח למשה רבינו דבר זה וכפירוש רש"י בד"ה העיני, אלמא
דשלוחא דבי דינא מותר לומר, הרי דלפירש"י העינן הזה קאי על לשון הרע,
והשליח היה יודע בעצמו שהדבר הזה הוא אמת שחרפוהו דתן ואבירם שאמרו
לו העיני האנשים ההם תנקר, כאדם שתולה קללתו בחבירו וכדפרש"י בחומש,
ואפילו הכי משמע בהדיא מהגמרא דאי לאו שלוחא דבי דינא היה אסור לספר.

Yad Dovid

b. presumably the emissary reported this to Moshe: This is clear since
the next verse states: "Moshe became very angry" (*Maharsha*). Moreover,
the emissary must have been permitted to tell Moshe; for if the emissary's
report was a transgression of *loshon hora*, Moshe Rabbeinu would not
have written it in the Torah (*Meiras Einayim* to *Choshen Mishpat* 8:24).

c. a question of loshon hora: Since the emissary reported how he was
personally insulted.

d. the eyes of those men: As *Rashi* in his commentary to the *Chumash*
explains, they meant themselves, but spoke of other people's eyes being
put out, like a man who attributes to his fellow the curse which should
come upon himself.

e. only because he was an emissary of the Beis Din: Because he was an
emissary of the *beis din*, he had a *to'eles* (constructive purpose) in telling
the court about the insult; for the litigant's sharp refusal is evidence of his
attitude — and the *beis din* need to know about this in order to respond
appropriately. Thus, one who is not an emissary of the *beis din* would be
forbidden to relate that someone insulted him, unless there is a distinct
to'eles in relating the information (see below, ch. 10); for when there is a
constructive purpose — in addition to the other conditions mentioned
below in ch. 10, clause 2 — relating the information is not considered to be
loshon hora.

Rosh and *Ran* adopt a different text of this Gemara,[a] according to which the emissary did not tell the *beis din*: ["He insulted me," but "He insulted you."] If so, the prohibition would not be *loshon hora*, but *rechilus* — inciting the *beis din* to hate the litigant, as we shall explain below.[b] However, *Rosh* and *Ran*, like *Rashi* derive from this Gemara that, except for an emissary of the *beis din*, the prohibition applies even if the information is true.[c] Moreover, it is clear that according to *Rosh* and *Ran* this principle applies not only to *rechilus*, but also to *loshon hora*.[d]

Thus, according to all, *loshon hora* is forbidden even if it is true.

Further proof can be adduced from Tractate *Sotah* (42a), where the Gemara lists four classes of people who do not merit to greet the *Shechinah* [i.e. the Divine Presence does not rest upon them]. The list includes the class of liars and the class of those who speak *loshon hora*. If *loshon hora* were forbidden only when it is false, why would the Gemara list these as two separate classes?[e] This proof is given by Rabbeinu Yonah in *Shaarei Teshuvah* [3:214].

A further proof can be found in *Bava Basra* (164b), which relates: "A folded and sewn deed came before Rebbe, and upon examining it he said: 'There is no date [written] in this!' [Rabbi Shimon the son of Rebbe said: 'Perhaps it [the date] is [written] in between the sewn fold?' (Rebbe) cut the sewing and saw the date] and then looked angrily at him.] He [Rabbi Shimon] said to him: 'I did not write it; Rabbi Yehuda Chayata wrote it.' [Rebbe] said to him [Rabbi Shimon]: 'Stop speaking this *loshon hora*.'" *Rashbam* explains that Rebbe was telling his son, Rabbi Shimon: 'You should not have mentioned that Rabbi Yehudah Chayata was at fault,[g] but should simply have said, 'I did not write it.' Thus it is forbidden to report disparaging information about someone even if it is true, and this is termed *loshon hora*.

Yad Dovid

a. a different text of this Gemara: This text is cited below, ch. 2, *Be'er Mayim Chaim* , clause 2,.s.v. "ועוד ראיה ממימרא דרבא"

b. as we shall explain below: Ch. 2, *Be'er Mayim Chaim* , clause 2. Also in *Hilchos Rechilus*, Ch. 1, *Be'er Mayim Chaim*, clause 8.

ואפילו לפי גירסת הרא"ש והר"ן דהענין הזה איירי ברכילות כמו שנבאר לקמן, מכל מקום לענין דינא לא מצינו שיחלקו על פירש"י, דכי היכי דלדידהו איירי הגמרא לענין רכילות ועל-כרחך דאסור אפילו על אמת אי לאו שלוחא דבי דינא וכמו שנבאר אי"ה לקמן בתחלת חלק שני, כן הוא הדין בלשון הרע. הרי דאיסור לשון הרע הוא אפילו על אמת.

ועוד ראיה מדחשב בסוטה בסוף פרק אלו נאמרין ד' כיתות שאינם מקבלים פני שכינה ובתוכם כת שקרנים כת מספרי לשון הרע ואי לשון הרע אינו אסור רק בשקר אמאי חשב להו בשתים כמו שכתב רבינו יונה ראיה זו בשערי תשובה (מאמר רי"ד). ועוד ראיה מדאיתא בבבא בתרא (קס"ד ע"ב) ההוא שטר מקושר דאתא לקמיה דרבי, אמר רבי אין זמן בזה וכו' הדר חזא ביה רבי בבישות אמר ליה לאו אנא כתבתיה ר' יהודא חייטא כתביה, אמר ליה רבי לר' שמעון בריה כלך מלשון הרע הזה, ופירש רשב"ם לא היה לך להטיל האשמה עליו אלא היה לך לומר איני כתבתיו. הרי דאף על אמת אסור לספר בגנות חבירו ונקרא לשון הרע.

Yad Dovid

c. **the prohibition applies even if the information is true:** *Hilchos Rechilus,* ch.1, clause 4, and *Be'er Mayim Chaim* there, clause 8.

d. **not only to rechilus, but also to loshon hora:** *Rechilus* can also be referred to as *loshon hora* (see *Hilchos Loshon Hora,,* ch. 2, *Be'er Mayim Chaim,* clause 3, s.v. "היוצא מדבריו", *Hilchos Rechilus* ch. 3, *Be'er Mayim Chaim,* clause 2; ch.8, *Be'er Mayim Chaim,* clause 6.)

e. **why would the Gemara list these as two separate classes?** If the prohibition of *loshon hora* applied only to false information, those who speak *loshon hora* would anyway be denied the merit to greet the *Shechinah* since they would be in the class of liars.

f. **looked angrily at him:** Rebbe did not approve of the way the deed had been prepared, and was angry at Rabbi Shimon because he thought he had written it, since R' Shimon now appeared to know where the date was written (*Rashbam*).

g. **'you should not have mentioned that Rabbi Yehudah Chayata was at fault:'** From this we see Rebbe held that even assuming R' Yehuda Chayata truly had written it, it would be *loshon hora* for R' Shimon to reveal it. This shows that a derogatory statement is *loshon hora* even if it is true.

All the early halachic authorites [*Rishonim*] state clearly that *loshon hora* is forbidden even if the information is true. (The latter authorities, *Acharonim*, also state this, but the citations are so numerous that there is no room for them here.) For example, *Rambam* states in his commentary to *Avos* (1:17): "*Loshon Hora* does not mean that one lies about someone, attributing to him something he did not do; for this is in the category of *motzi shem ra*. Rather, *loshon hora* means revealing disparaging information about a person, even about deeds that he *really performed*. The one who relates such information commits a sin, and the one who listens to it commits a sin." *Rambam* reiterates this in *Hilchos De'os* (7:2). The same ruling is given by *Sefer Mitzvos Gadol* in Negative Precepts, clause 9, and by Rabbeinu Yonah in *Sha'arei Teshuvah* [3:214]. It is also implied in the commentaries of *Rashi* and *Ramban* to *Vayikra* 19:16.

I have gone into great detail on this point. If only Hashem would grant that these words would help somewhat to remove this blindness[a] from people's hearts!

(2) [to *Mekor HaChaim*, clause 1, p. 112] **An Admixture of untruth:** The Gemara in *Shevuos* (31a) gives several examples of untruth to which it applies the verse: "Keep far away from a false matter" (*Shemos* 23:7). All these examples imply that truth mixed with a small amount of untruth is forbidden by the Torah just as total untruth is forbidden. And especially concerning *loshon hora* and *rechilus*, it is known that by changing just one word[b] in one's report of the facts one can change the whole significance of those facts.

(3) [to *Mekor HaChaim*, clause 1, p. 114] **"You shall not go as a talebearer among your people:"** So writes *Rambam* (*Hilchos De'os* 7:2) and *Sefer Mitzvos Gadol* (Negative Precepts, clause 9). The following are the words [of *Rambam*] :

Yad Dovid

a. this blindness: The error of thinking that *loshon hora* is permitted if it is true.

וכן איתא להדיא בכל הפוסקים הראשונים (מלבד ספרי האחרונים קצרה היריעה
מהכילם) דלשון הרע אסור אפילו על אמת. דזה לשון הרמב"ם בפרק א' דאבות
שאין לשון הרע שיכזב על האדם וייחס לו מה שלא יעשה כי זה נקרא מוציא
שם רע על חבירו, ואמנם לשון הרע הוא שיגלה גנות האדם אפילו בפעולותיו
אשר יעשה באמת, שהאומרו יחטא ואשר ישמעהו יחטא עכ"ל הטהור. וכן כתב
הרמב"ם בפרק ז' מהלכות דיעות הלכה ב'. והסמ"ג לאוין ט. והרבינו יונה
בשערי תשובה במאמר רי"ד. וכן משמע מפירוש רש"י בחומש פרשת קדושים
על זה הפסוק דלא תלך רכיל ע"ש. וכן משמע בפירוש הרמב"ן על זה הפסוק
עי"ש. והארכתי הרבה אולי יתן ה' שיועיל קצת להוציא את העוורון הזה מלבות
בני אדם.

(ב) תערובות. כן משמע בשבועות (ל"א א.) בכל הציורים שהביא שם הגמרא
על הפסוק מדבר שקר תרחק דתערובות של שקר במקצת אסרה התורה כמו עצם
השקר, ובפרט בענין לשון הרע ורכילות ידוע הוא דעל ידי תיבה אחת שנשתנה
בהספור נשתנה הענין כולו.

(ג) לא תלך וכו'. כן כתב הרמב"ם בפרק ז' מהלכות דיעות, והסמ"ג, שזה
לשונו:

Yad Dovid

b. changing just one word : In order to commit the sin of *motzi shem ra*
one need not falsify the entire report; even one untrue word makes it *motzi
shem ra*, since it changes the impression made by the report as a whole.
Thus *Chofetz Chaim* here has derived this halachic point about *motzi shem
ra* (a prohibition derived from "You shall not go about as a talebearer;" see
below, *Be'er Mayim Chaim* , clause 3) from what we find concerning the
prohibition of "Keep far away from a false matter."

It should be noted that even if one's entire account is accurate, it is still
motzi shem ra if one omits a detail and the omission gives a disparaging
effect. For example, if one relates that Reuven struck or insulted Shimon,
but omits to state the initial provocation on Shimon's part, this would be
motzi shem ra. (*Ohev Yamim*, ch. 16, clause 6.)

"There is a sin much greater than [rechilus],[a] and it is included in [i.e. deduced from] this negative precept [against rechilus]; and this [greater sin] is when one speaks disparagingly about another, even though one is telling the truth..."

This statement of Rambam might seem to be contradicted by the Gemara in Kesubos (46a) which only mentions that our verse is a warning against the sin of motzi shem ra [but does not mention that it is a warning against rechilus or loshon hora]. Now, motzi shem ra is the most serious offense of all, since it is a lie, while loshon hora and rechilus by definition are true statements. [Thus one might think that the warning against rechilus and loshon hora cannot be deduced from our verse, which only warns against the more serious offense.] In fact, however, this Gemara does not contradict the statement of Rambam; for this Gemara, in mentioning motzi shem ra, did not intend to exclude rechilus and loshon hora.

This can be proven from the Gemara in Sanhedrin (29a), [where a Mishnah gives details of the procedure that the beis din follows in judging property disputes. After the witnesses have been interrogated, the judges discuss the case privately among themselves, and after reaching their verdict they call in the defendant and tell him: 'You are acquitted' or 'You are liable to pay.' Then the Mishnah asks:] "From where do we derive that when one of the judges [emerges from the courtroom] he may not say: 'I was for acquital, [but what could I do? My colleages were in the majority and maintained   you are liable?'"[b] The Mishnah answers:] "We derive it from the Torah's statement: 'You shall not go about as a talebearer among your people.'" [From this Gemara it is clear that this verse constitutes a warning against rechilus.]

Likewise the fact that our verse refers [not only to motzi shem ra but also] to rechilus and loshon hora, is clearly indicated in Sifra (Parashas Kedoshim) and the Jerusalem Talmud (Pe'ah 1:1) where Chazal say that the word "talebearer" (רוֹכֵל) is related to "peddler" (רָכִיל) because [in speaking loshon hora and rechilus] the talebearer is like a peddler who goes around picking things up in one place and selling them in another.

יש עון גדול מזה עד מאוד והוא בכלל לאו זה והוא המספר בגנות חבירו אף על
פי שאומר אמת וכו'. ואף דבכתובות (מ"ו ע"א) לא נזכר רק דהוא אזהרה
למוציא שם רע שהוא חמור מכל מפני שהוא דבר שקר, מכל מקום אין כונת
הגמרא להוציא סתם לשון הרע ורכילות שהוא אפילו על אמת מכלל זה, שהרי
בסנהדרין כ"ט (ע"א) במשנה אמרו מנין לדיין וכו' שלא יאמר אני מזכה כו'
תלמוד לומר לא תלך רכיל בעמיך, ובספרא פרשת קדושים ובירושלמי פרק א'
דפאה איתא בהדיא הלאו על לשון הרע ורכילות ממש שהוא כרוכל שמטעין
דברים מזה לזה.

Yad Dovid

a. much greater than [rechilus] : The reason why *loshon hora* is a more
severe sin than *rechilus* is explained below *Be'er Mayim Chaim*, clause 4.

b. maintained you are liable: This judge is speaking *rechilus* because he
creates animosity between the defendant and the other judges. Since his
statement is true, it is considered to be *rechilus* rather than *motzi shem ra*
(see Overview, para. 4).

And see part 2, ch. 1, *Be'er Mayim Chaim,* clause 8.[a] Thus the Gemara in *Kesubos* does not mean that our verse refers only to *motzi shem ra,* but rather that since the verse prohibits *loshon hora* and *rechilus* [which are less severe than *motzi shem ra*], it certainly also prohibits *motzi shem ra.*

(4) [to *Mekor HaChaim,* clause 1, p. 114] **And this [verse prohibits *loshon hora,* since *loshon hora* is included in this prohibition of *rechilus*:]** *Rambam* (*Hilchos De'os* 7:2) writes that the prohibition against *loshon hora* is included in this verse about *rechilus.* He means that the prohibition of *loshon hora* can be deduced by *kal vechomer (a fortiori)* from that of *rechilus;* for if *rechilus,* which is not necessarily disparaging, is forbidden, then all the more so *loshon hora,*[b] which is disparaging!

Ravad, on the other hand, maintains that *rechilus* is worse than *loshon hora*[c] (*Hasagos* to *Hilchos De'os* 7:2). Thus he maintains that the prohibition of *loshon hora* cannot be deduced by *kal vechomer* from that of *rechilus.* If so, from where does *Ravad* derive the prohibition of *loshon hora*?

We can say that he derives it from the verse: "You shall not carry a false report"[d] (*Shemos* 23:1); for the Gemara in *Pesachim* (118a) expounds this verse: "Do not read לֹא תִשָּׂא ["you shall not carry"], but לֹא תַשִּׂיא ['You shall not cause others to carry']; i.e. You shall not speak *loshon hora* [thus causing others to "carry" (accept) it].

In addition, *Ravad* could derive the prohibition from the verse: "Cursed be he who smites his fellow Jew in secret" (*Devorim* 27: 24)

Yad Dovid

a. It is clear that this source has nothing to do with the subject matter discussed here; therefore either there is a line missing in the text of *Be'er Mayim Chaim* or the source is a printing error.

b. all the more so loshon hora: The source of *Chofetz Chaim* is from what *Kesef Mishneh* writes at the beginning of ch. 7 of *Hilchos De'os* (and see Overview, paras. 15-16). An alternative explanation is given by *Radvaz* (vol. 2, *siman* 1374), who explains that when someone speaks *rechilus* (e.g.,

ועיין בחלק ב' כלל א' בבאר מים חיים סעיף קטן ח', רק דכוונת הגמרא
בכתובות הוא במכל-שכן דמוציא שם רע מכלל לאו זה לא נפקא.

(ד) וזה. כן כתב הרמב"ם שם וכוונתו דכל-שכן הוא כיון שמבזיהו בסיפור זה,
ולהראב"ד בהשגות שסובר דרכילות חמור מלשון הרע נוכל לומר דלדידיה
נפקא-ליה לשון הרע מקרא דלא תשא, קרי ביה לא תשיא, אזהרה למספר לשון
הרע כמו שכתוב בפסחים (קי"ח ע"א). וגם מקרא דארור מכה רעהו בסתר שהוא
קאי על לשון הרע כמו דפירש רש"י בחומש.

Yad Dovid

he tells someone what another has said about him or done to him), he
does so in hope of personal gain, expecting to receive some payment or
favor from the person he informs. [Therefore he is more overpowered by
his evil inclination to commit the sin; and hence the punishment is less.]
But one who speaks *loshon hora* has no expectation of personal gain; hence
his punishment is more severe (see above, Introduction, "Negative
Precepts," *Mekor HaChaim*, clause 6; and for further discussion of this view
of *Radvaz see Sefer Nesivos Chaim, Zera Chaim*, p. 278, in the *Hagoh*).

c. rechilus is worse than loshon hora: According to *Ravad* , *rechilus* is
worse than *loshon hora* because *rechilus* results in the death of three people
— the speaker, the one who accepts the report, and the one spoken about
— while *loshon hora* results in the death of only one person, the speaker
himself. *Rambam*, on the other hand, maintains that *loshon hora* also can
result in the death of three people, but it is worse than *rechilus* because it
involves disparagement of another person, as explained in the preceding
comment of *Yad Dovid* (and see Overview, para. 16). The disagreement
between *Rambam* and *Ravad* is based on their differing interpretations of
the Gemara in *Erachin* (15b) (*Kesef Mishneh, Hilchos De'os* 7:2; for more
commentary on that Gemara passage, see *Rashi* and *Tosafos* there;
Jerusalem Talmud, *Pe'ah* 1:1, p. 4b and *Pnei Moshe* ad loc.; *Shaarei
Teshuvah* by Rabbeinu Yonah, ch. 3, clause 222; *Kesef Mishneh*, loc. cit.).

d. a false report: This translation of the verse follows Onkelos. For
discussion of how this can refer to *loshon hora* if the derogatory
information is true, see above, Negative Precepts, *Be'er Mayim Chaim*,
clause 2,.s.v. "ואעפ"כ קראתו התורה שמע שוא".

which refers to *loshon hora*, as *Rashi* explains there[a].

Ravad could also derive the prohibition from the verse: "Remember what Hashem your God did to Miriam"[b] (*Devorim* 24:9), which is commanded by the Torah in order that we should be careful not to speak *loshon hora*, as is mentioned in *Sifri*, and as explained above [Positive Precepts, clause 1]. *

HAGOH [c]

If we assume that *Ravad* could derive the prohibition of *loshon hora* from the verse: "You shall not carry a false report" [see above], the following question arises: Since [according to *Ravad*] *rechilus* is worse than *loshon hora*, why did the Torah need to write a separate verse prohibiting *rechilus* [i.e., "You shall not go about as a talebearer"]? Why not just derive this prohibition by *kal vechomer [a fortiori]* from the verse prohibiting *loshon hora* ?

The answer is that the Torah wanted to give a specific negative precept against *loshon hora* ["You shall not carry a false report"], and [another against] *rechilus* ["You shall not go about as a talebearer"], thus making it possible for the *beis din* to give a lashing for the sin of *motzi shem ra* [false slander], as explained by the Gemara[d] in *Kesubos* (46a). If the only source of the prohibition against *loshon hora* [and, *kal vechomer, rechilus*] were the verse: "You shall not carry a false report," no lashing could be given, for that verse includes a different prohibition.[e]

There is another possible reason why [according to *Ravad*] the Torah writes: "You shall not go about as a talebearer" — namely, to inform us that one transgresses the prohibition against *rechilus* from the moment he picks up his feet to go and commit the sin. This is similar to what we find in Tractate *Avodah Zarah* (18b): ["Rabbi Shimon ben Pazi expounded as follows: What is meant by the verse: 'Happy is the man] who has not walked [in the counsel of the wicked nor stood in the way of sinners, nor sat among scorners' (*Tehillim* 1:1)? If he did not walk that way at all,

142

באר מים חיים

ומקרא דזכור את אשר עשה ה' אלהיך למרים שהוא כדי שנזהר מלשון הרע
כדאיתא בספרי כמו שביארנו לעיל בפתיחה.*
*הגה"ה.
ולפירוש זה צריך לומר מה שפרטה התורה לאו על רוכל ולא סמכה
(להראב"ד שסובר דרכילות חמור מלשון הרע) במכל-שכן על לאו דלא
תשיא וכנ"ל, משום דהתורה רצתה להשמיענו לאו מיוחד לאיסור לשון
הרע ורכילות ונפקא מיניה שיהא חייב מלקות במוציא שם רע כמו

Yad Dovid

a. as Rashi explains there: For a discussion of why the verse is interpreted
as referring to **loshon hora,** see below, ch. 3, clause 1.

b. what Hashem your God did to Miriam: She was punished with
leprosy because she was considered to have spoken *loshon hora* about
Moshe Rabbeinu. For discussion of the episode see below, ch.8, *Be'er
Mayim Chaim,* clause 1, with *Hagoh.*

c. Hagoh: Throughout *Sefer Chofetz Chaim,* the author (*Chofetz Chaim*)
occasionally inserted additional comments under the title: *Hagoh*
(meaning "note" or "comment"). This particular *Hagoh* belongs here (as is
clear from the context), and not as printed in earlier editions of *Sefer
Chofetz Chaim.* (See *Sefer Chofetz Chaim, Kol Haloshon* ed. Jerusalem, 5754
(1984), p. 78.

d. as explained by the Gemara: The Gemara there states if a man falsely
slanders his bride (claiming that he found her to have committed
adultery), he is subject to lashing.

Now, the rule is there can be no punishment of lashing unless the
Torah gives a specific warning against the prohibition: אֵין עוֹנְשִׁין אֶלָּא אִם כֵּן
מַזְהִירִין (see *Sanhedrin* 56b). In our case, says the Gemara in *Kesubos* , the
warning against *motzi shem ra* is the verse: "You shall not go about as a
talebearer." As explained above, this verse refers to *rechilus*, and all the
more so, *motzi shem ra*. (*Motzi shem ra* is derived by *kal vechomer* from
rechilus: If *rechilus* is forbidden even though the information conveyed is
true, then all the more so *motzi shem ra*, where the information is a lie!)

e. includes a different prohibition: The rule is that a prohibition stated in
an "inclusive verse" (לָאו שֶׁבִּכְלָלוֹת, a verse including two or more different

how could he stand there? And if he did not stand there he obviously did not sit among them; and since he did not sit among them, he could not have scorned! But the verse teaches you] that if one walks [towards the wicked he will subsequently stand with them, and if he stands, he will in the end sit with them, and if he sits he will also come to scorn. "[a]]

It is also similar to the Gemara in *Avodah Zarah* (8a), [which discusses the verse from which we derive the prohibition against attending the banquets (weddings, etc.) of idolators: "Lest you make a covenant with the (idolatrous) inhabitants of the land...and sacrifice to their gods], and one of them invite you, [and you eat of his sacrifice" (*Shemos* 34:15). The Gemara asks: "Doesn't this prohibition apply only if one actually eats of their sacrifice?" Rava answers: "If this were so the verse would only have said: 'and you eat of his sacrifice.' Why then say: 'and one of them invite you?' It is to inform us] that from the time he invites you it is considered as if everything you ate was from his sacrifice. "

Similarly in *Bava Metzia* (61b) [the Gemara cites the verse:] "You shall not do unrighteousness...in weights" (*Vayikra* 19:35), [and the Gemara asks: Why is this verse necessary? After all, the Torah has already prohibited stealing, the use of false weights is just a form of stealing! The answer is: To inform us] that one transgresses the prohibition from the moment he makes the false weights, even though he has not yet weighed anything with them.

So too our verse might come to inform us that from the moment one prepares himself to go and speak *rechilus* he transgresses the prohibition.

After writing this, I found the same idea in *Shnei Luchos Habris (Sheloh)*. [See *Sheloh, Torah Sheb'kesav, Parashas Kedoshim — Derech Chaim*, p. 201.]

end of *HAGOH*

שאמרו בכתובות (מ"ו ע"א) דלא תשא תשמע שוא כולל נמי ענין אחר
כמו דאיתא בשבועות ל"א בגמרא עי"ש וכמו שכתבנו לעיל בפתיחה
בלאוין אות ב'. או אפשר דהתורה רצתה להשמיענו שיש לו איסור
משעת הילוכו שהקדים רגליו לדבר עבירה וכעין מה שאמרו בע"ז
(יח:) אשר לא הלך כיון שהלך וכו' שהלך וכו' וכעין שאמרו שם (ח.)
וקרא לך כיון שקרא לך נעשה כאלו אכלת מזבחו, ובבא מציעא (ס"א:)
לא תעשו עול במשקל לעבור עליו משעת עשייה ואפילו לא שקל בהן
עדיין, וכן כאן כיון שהזמין עצמו לילך ולדבר רכילות עובר על לאו זה.
אחר כך מצאתי זה בשל"ה.

סוף הגה"ה

Yad Dovid

prohibitions) cannot serve as the basis for lashing. (See *Sanhedrin* 63a;
Shevuos 31a; and above, Negative Precepts, *Be'er Mayim Chaim*, clause 2.)

One might ask: If so, how can the verse: "You shall not go about as a
talebearer" serve as the basis for lashing? After all, it contains two
prohibitions — *rechilus* and *motzi shem ra*! The answer is that since these
two are closely related (i.e. they are simply two types of evil speech), this
verse is not considered "inclusive." For further discussion of this point see
Nesivos Chaim, pp. 289-90. However, the verse "You shall not carry a false
report" includes a prohibition unrelated to *loshon hora* as mentioned in
Shevuos 31a and therefore is an inclusive verse and cannot serve as a basis
for lashing.

a. he will also come to scorn: *Chofetz Chaim* understands that the moment
one walks towards the wicked, it is accounted to him as if he is already
among them. For discussion of this point see *Nesivos Chaim*, p. 295.

On the other hand, *Ravad* might derive the prohibition from the verse about *rechilus* ("You shall not go about as a talebearer...") [but not as a *kal vachomer* deduction]. *Rashi* in his commentary to this verse explains that "talebearer" refers to someone who goes into other people's houses to spy, hoping to see or hear something bad so that he can go and tell it in the street. Thus [even without *Rambam's kal vechomer* reasoning] *Rashi* includes both *loshon hora* and *rechilus* in the term "talebearer;"[a] and *Ravad* might adopt this same interpretation.

Rashi will understand that when the Midrash in *Toras Kohanim* [*Kedoshim Parashasa* 2, ch. 4, clause 5] states that a talebearer carries reports "from this one to that one"[b] it means from the householder ("this one") to any other person ("that one").[c] [Thus the verse refers not only to *rechilus* but also to *loshon hora.*] This is in contrast to *Rambam* [*Hilchos De'os* 7:2], who explains that the wording of the Midrash: "from this one to that one" means: "one who carries bad words to the person about whom they were spoken". [Thus the verse explicitly refers to *rechilus* alone[d] and the prohibition of *loshon hora* must be deduced by *kal vechomer* from that of *rechilus*].

Yad Dovid

a. both loshon hora and rechilus in the term "talebearer": The talebearer finds out what evil the householder has to say about so-and-so. He then goes and "tells it in the street." Thus he does not go directly to the person the householder spoke about; rather, it first becomes a matter that is likely to become public knowledge (מִלְּתָא דַעֲבִידָתָא לְגָלוּיֵי) and hence will eventually reach the ears of the one about whom it was spoken. When the talebearer first related it to others, that was *loshon hora* . When it comes to the attention of the one spoken about, it is *rechilus.* Thus the word "talebearer" includes both transgressions.

b. from this one to that one: The wording "this one to that one" is not found in *Toras Kohanim,* but is in the text of the Jerusalem Talmud, *Pe'ah* 1:1 (p. 4b).

146

או סובר כפירוש רש״י בחומש, דהרוכל מקרי מי שהולך לבית רעהו לרגל אולי
יראה או ישמע דבר רע ויספר בשוק, והנה כלל הרוכל והמספר לשון הרע ביחד
במלת רוכל. וכוונת התורת כהנים במה שאמר שמטעין דברים מזה לזה היינו
מאיש זה לאיש אחר, ולא כמו לפירוש הרמב״ם דכוונת התו״כ היינו שמטעין
למי שדיבר המדבר עליו מתחלה דהיינו רכילות.

Yad Dovid

c. to any other person ("that one"): This is how *Ravad* explains *Toras
Kohanim*, loc. cit.

d. rechilus alone: *Rambam's* interpretation is different from *Rashi's* .
According to *Rambam* , the talebearer mentioned in the verse is one who
goes directly to the person spoken about and tells him what the
householder said about him (See above, Negative Precepts, clause 1). This
implies that if he told it in the street (as *Rashi* interpreted), so that it comes
only indirectly to the attention of the one spoken about, this is not
considered *rechilus* (see *Marpeh Loshon*, pamphlet 6, p. 7).

[It was suggested above that, even without *Rambam's kal vechomer* argument, *Ravad* might derive the prohibition against *loshon hora* from the verse about *rechilus* ("You shall not go about as a talebearer..."), by interpreting the term "talebearer" as including both *loshon hora* and *rechilus.*]

Similarly *Ramban* in his commentary to the *Chumash* implies that the term "talebearer" includes both [*loshon hora* and *rechilus;*] for he explains that a talebearer is like a peddler who circulates constantly, buying here and selling there;[a] and this is why the Torah adds the expression: "among your people" ("You shall not go about as a talebearer among your people") — to emphasize that the talebearer walks about among the public, hearing from all and telling to all.[b]

Similarly, the Jerusalem Talmud (*Pe'ah* , ch. 1) implies that our verse refers both to *loshon hora* and to *rechilus.* [c]

[In summary: *Ravad* takes issue with *Rambam's* opinion that the prohibition against *loshon hora* is derived by *kal vechomer (a fortiori)* from the verse: "You shall not go about as a talebearer..." It could be that *Ravad* derives the prohibition against *loshon hora* from other verses; or it could be that he derives it from this very verse, but not through *kal vechomer* reasoning.

If *Ravad* derives the prohibition from other verses, how does he explain the necessity for our verse? The answer is that it may be needed in order to empower the *beis din* to administer lashing for the sin of *motzi shem ra.* Alternatively, the verse might be needed in order to extend the scope of the prohibition, so that not only the actual speaking of *rechilus* is forbidden, but even the preparation to do so.]

Yad Dovid

a. **buying here and selling there:** *Ramban* implies that after the talebearer hears a householder speak badly about someone, he goes and repeats his gossip to anyone he can, not just to the one about whom the householder spoke. Thus the verse refers not only to *rechilus* (telling the one who was spoken about) but also *loshon hora* (telling others).

באר מים חיים

וכן מפירוש הרמב"ן בחומש משמע דתיבת רוכל כולל שניהם, שכן פירש שם
שרוכל הוא ההולך כל היום וקונה מכאן ומכאן והולך ומוכר במקומות אחרים
בכאן ובכאן, כן הוא הרוכל הזה, ולזה בא תיבת בעמיך לרמוז כי הוא הולך
ברבים כדי שיהיה לו מה לשמוע ולרגל אחר כך עי"ש. וכן משמע בירושלמי
פרק א' דפיאה שהוא אזהרה ללשון הרע ורכילות ועיין שם בפני משה בד"ה תני
ר' נחמיה.

Yad Dovid

b. **And telling to all:** [The position of *Ramban* on this issue is not
completely clear, for] in his commentary to *Parashas Ki Setze* (*Devorim*
24:9) he implies that the term "talebearer" refers only to [*rechilus* and not
to *loshon hora*]. (*Hagoh* — emendation — printed in *Sefer Chofetz Chaim*,
at the end of *Hilchos Rechilus*. The text of that *Hagoh* contains a
misprint; it should read "...only to *rechilus*;" see above, Positive
Precepts, *Be'er Mayim Chaim* , clause 1. s.v. "מזה משמע מדבריו")
c. **both to loshon hora and to rechilus:** See *Pnei Moshe* there, s.v. תני רבי
נחמיה

(5) [to *Mekor HaChaim* , clause 3, p. 116] **Like those who are accustomed always to sit and say:** This is clearly stated in *Rambam* (*Hilchos De'os* 7:2) and *Kesef Mishneh* there.

(6) [to *Mekor HaChaim* , clause 4, p. 118] **Chazal say:** This is the wording of *Rambam* (*Hilchos De'os* 7:3) and *Sefer Mitzvos Gadol* (Negative Precepts 9). Their source is *Tosefta Pe'ah* 1:2; and almost the entire statement is also mentioned in the Babylonian Talmud in *Erachin* [15b] (see there). However, the passage in *Erachin* states only that *loshon hora* is more stringent[a] than idolatry, forbidden relations, and murder. It is the *Tosefta* which adds that the transgressor has no share in the world to come.[b]

This matter is also mentioned in the Jerusalem Talmud, *Pe'ah* 1:1. However, the text there is somewhat different, for it states: "There are three sins for which a person is punished in this world, but the main punishment is reserved for the world to come,[c] and *loshon hora* is equivalent to all of them." However, both [the Jerusalem Talmud and *Tosefta*] are making the same point; for in the case of idolatry and the like, if one does not confess [i.e. repent], he has no share in the world to come, even though he is put to death by the *beis din*. This is implied by the Mishnah in *Sanhedrin* [43b], which states that when a person is executed for one of these sins he is told: "Confess; for all who confess have a share in the world to come."[d] All the more so does this apply to *loshon hora*, for if one is habituated to this sin it is even more grave than the other three (as explained above). Thus if [as stated by the Jerusalem Talmud] the main punishment remains to be exacted in the world to come [i.e. if he does not confess], surely he also will have no share in that world. If so, the Jerusalem Talmud does not disagree

Yad Dovid

a. loshon hora is more stringent: Although the Gemara here states that one who speaks *loshon hora* is sinning as greatly as if he had committed these three sins, nevertheless the intent is not that *loshon hora* is more stringent, because the Torah does not mention a punishment of death for

(ה) שרגילין תמיד וכו'. כל זה הוא מבואר ברמב"ם ובכסף משנה שם.

(ו) אמרו חז"ל. לשון הרמב"ם שם, והסמ"ג לאוין ט', והוא בתוספתא דפאה, וכמעט כל המימרא איתא גם כן בערכין (טו ע"ב) בגמרא עי"ש. אך דבגמרא דידן איתא סתם שחמור מעבודה זרה וגילוי עריות ושפיכות דמים והתוספתא מבאר דאין לו חלק לעולם הבא. ודבר זה ישנו גם כן בירושלמי בפרק א' דפאה עי"ש, אך בירושלמי הוא קצת בנוסח אחר וזה לשונו על ג' עבירות נפרעין מן האדם בעולם הזה וחקרן קיימת לו לעולם הבא וכו' ולשון הרע נגד כולן. אבל הכל הולך אל מקום אחד, דכי היכי דעל עבודת כוכבים ומזלות וכיוצא בזה אם לא התודה אין לו חלק לעולם הבא אף שהמיתו אותו בבית דין כדמשמע בסנהדרין (מ"ג ע"ב) במשנה דאומרים לחייבי מיתות התודה שכן כל המתודה יש לו חלק לעולם הבא, ועל אחת כמה וכמה בלשון הרע אם הורגל בעון זה שחמור מזה, וכנ"ל, אם ישאר לו הקרן קיים לעולם הבא בודאי דלא יהיה לו גם כן חלק לעולם הבא, ואם כן אין הירושלמי חולק עם התוספתא ולכן יפה פסק הרמב"ם כהתוספתא.

Yad Dovid

committing the sin of *loshon hora* as it does with regard to these three sins. Rather the intent of the Gemara is that *loshon hora* can lead to committing severe sins (*Maharsha*, s.v. 'כל המספר לשון הרע מגדיל עוונות כנגד כו). Thus we find that even *Chofetz Chaim* states "and *loshon hora* is *equivalent* to all of them" as opposed to "*loshon hora* is more stringent etc." (see below , and *Mekor HaChaim* here).

b. has no share in the world to come: The text of our editions of the *Tosefta* does not mention that one has no share in the world to come but rather that the main punishment is reserved for the world to come (see *Sefer Avodas Hamelech* to *Rambam Hilchos De'os* 7:3 for discussion about this).

c. reserved for the world to come: This would seem to imply that although one is punished in the world to come, after the punishment he has a share in that world. Hence one might think that the Jerusalem Talmud contradicts the *Tosefta*, which stated that the transgressor has no share in the world to come. However, *Be'er Mayim Chaim* proceeds to reconcile the two.

d. a share in the world to come: This implies that one who does not confess has no share in the world to come.

151

with the *Tosefta* , and *Rambam* is correct in ruling in accord with *Tosefta.*[a]

When I wrote: "The *Rishonim* explain..." the reference was to Rabbeinu Yonah in *Shaarei Teshuvah,* in his *Hilchos Loshon Hora* [*maamar* 203]. The same interpretation is clearly implied by *Rambam* (*Hilchos Teshuvah* 3:6), where he lists those who have no share in the world to come and includes *baalei loshon hora.* He does not say 'those who speak *loshon hora,*' but *baalei loshon hora*; and I have already explained in the name of *Kesef Mishneh*[b] that this means those for whom this sin has become a permanent, brazen habit.

(7) [to *Mekor HaChaim,* clause 5, p. 118] **Insistent with him:** [This law is derived] from the story of Do'eg and King Shaul, as related in the First Book of *Shmuel.*

[King Shaul suspected Dovid of coveting the throne, and decided to kill him. Yehonasan, the King's son, informed Dovid of this and Dovid fled. He came to Nov, the city of Kohanim, where Achimelech the Kohen assisted him (ibid, ch. 21). Do'eg, the Head of the Sanhedrin, was present at Nov and saw this. Meanwhile King Shaul found out that Yehonasan had helped Dovid. The King assembled his closest ministers and advisors, including Do'eg, and berated them bitterly, accusing them of conspiring against him in hope of receiving bribes from Dovid. "All of you have conspired against me. Will the son of Yishay (i.e. Dovid) give every one of you fields and vineyards...and there is none that give me an intimation" (*I Shmuel* 22:7-8). [Why had none of them cared enough to inform him of the covenant between Dovid and Yehonasan? At this point Do'eg related to the King that he had seen Achimelech help Dovid by consulting the *Urim* and *Tumim* for him and giving him food and a sword. As a result, King Shaul executed Achimelech and all the *kohanim* of Nov.] Now even though Shaul was the king,[c] and [those] present were very afraid of him,[d] nevertheless wherever [the Talmud] refers to this event it always considers Do'eg

ומה שכתבתי ופירשו הראשונים, הוא הרבינו יונה בשערי תשובה בהלכות לשון
הרע שלו, וכן מוכח מדברי הרמב״ם בפרק ג' מהלכות תשובה הלכה ו' שפסק
שם אלו שאין להם חלק לעולם הבא וקחשיב גם כן בתוכם בעלי לשון הרע, הרי
שלא קאמר ומי שסיפר לשון הרע רק בעלי לשון הרע, וכבר הראיתי לך בסעיף
קטן הקודם בשם הכסף משנה לבאר החילוק שביניהם.

(ז) עמד עליו וכו'. ממה שמבואר בכתוב גבי מעשה דדואג שעמד עליו שאול,
כמה שכתוב בקרא, כולכם קשרתם עלי לכולכם יתן בן ישי שדות וכרמים וגו'
ואין גולה את אזני וכו', ואף ששאול מלך היה, והיה להם אימה גדולה ממנו,
ואף על פי כן נחשב בכל מקום דואג לרוכל על דבר זה, ומזה נלמוד דהוא הדין

Yad Dovid

a. In accord with the Tosefta: When the Jerusalem Talmud stated that
"the main punishment is reserved for the world to come," it did not mean
that the transgressor has a share in that world. It only meant that the sin is
so grave that no punishment in this world would be sufficient to effect
atonement. But the main punishment is that, unless he repents, he will
have no share in the world to come. Thus the *Tosefta* simply states explicitly that which was implied by the Jerusalem Talmud. All these sources
— the Babylonian Talmud, the *Tosefta*, *Rambam*, and *Sefer Mitzvos Gadol* —
are in agreement that if one is in the habit of intentionally speaking *loshon
hora* he is in the class of *baalei loshon hora*, and if he does not repent he has
no share in the world to come.

b. in the name of Kesef Mishneh: Above, *Be'er Mayim Chaim*, clause 5.

c. Shaul was the king: And one is obligated to honor and revere a king of
Israel even more than one's father or rebbe (below, *Be'er Mayim Chaim*,
clause 8).

d. very afraid of him: Although the king was angry, he was not accusing
them of a capital offense, for if he were, it would have been permissible
for Do'eg to relate the information, since one does not have to give up
one's life in order to avoid speaking *loshon hora* (as explained above,
Mekor HaChaim, clause 4, *Yad Dovid*, s.v. "habituated to commit this sin
constantly" p. 118). Rather, they were afraid that the king would remove
them from their position. In such a case, one is obligated to give up his
position, if necessary, rather than speak *loshon hora* (*Ali Be'er* to *Be'er
Mayim Chaim* here; and see above, *Mekor HaChaim*, clause 6).

as guilty of *rechilus*[a] From this we may deduce that the same applies to *loshon hora* [I.e., even if someone whom one is obligated to honor and revere is urging him to relate certain facts, one is forbidden to do so if the report would include *loshon hora.*]

In any case [even without relying on the above proof from the story of Do'eg] this law is obvious, as we shall write below [*Be'er Mayim Chaim*, clause 8] regarding one's father or rebbe.

(8) [to *Mekor HaChaim*, clause 5, p. 118] **His father or his rebbe:** This is obvious, for *Shulchan Aruch* (*Yoreh De'ah* 240:15) states that if one's father commands him to transgress even a Rabbinic commandment, one must not obey him. And the same certainly applies to one's rebbe. In fact the Gemara goes even further, for it states that even if one sees his rebbe dressed in *kilayim* [a forbidden combination of linen and wool] one is required to tear the forbidden clothing off his rebbe, even in the street. Why? Because where there is desecration of the Divine Name [such as wearing *kilayim*], we do not take the honor of a rebbe into consideration [*Berachos* 19b]. And this is cited as Halachah in *Yoreh De'ah* [303:1]. Likewise if one sees one's rebbe transgressing any other prohibition, even a Rabbinic prohibition, one is required to protest to him, as explained in *Yoreh De'ah* [*Hagoh* to 242:22]. If so, it follows *a fortiori* that if one's rebbe commands one to transgress a prohibition, one should not obey him.

This can be proven from the Gemara in *Shevuos* [31a] which states that if one's rebbe asks him to commit even a hint of a falsehood, one is forbidden to do so; for the Gemara there says: "In the case of a Torah scholar whose rebbe says to him: 'You know that I would not lie even for ten thousand *dinar*. Now, a certain person owes me a hundred *dinar* [and denies the debt], and I have only one witness,[b]— From where do we learn that he [the student] may not join with him [the first witness? We learn this] from the verse: "Keep far from a falsehood" [*Shemos* 23:7].

154

לענין לשון הרע, ובלאו הכי הדבר פשוט כמו שנכתוב לקמן גבי אביו ורבו.

(ח) אביו או רבו. פשוט ממה דמבואר ביורה דעה בסימן ר"מ סעי' ט"ו דאם
אמר לו אביו לעבור אפילו על מצוה של דבריהם לא ישמע לו, והוא הדין בודאי
גבי רבו, ויותר מזה מצינו בברכות (דף י"ט ע"ב) ונפסק כן ביורה דעה סימן ש"ג
ס"א דאפילו אם רואה את רבו שהוא לובש כלאים צריך לפשוט ממנו אפילו
בשוק, מאי טעמא במקום שיש חילול השם אין חולקין כבוד לרב, וכן שאר דבר
איסור אם ראה לרבו שעובר אפילו על איסור דרבנן צריך למחות בידו כמבואר
ביורה דעה בסימן רמ"ב סכ"ב בהגה"ה, וא"כ כל-שכן שאין צריך לשמוע לו
לעשות איסור. וכן מוכח בשבועות (דף לא ע"א), דאפילו גרא דשקר אסור
לציית לרבו, דזה לשון הגמרא שם, מנין לתלמיד שאמר לו רבו יודע אתה בי
שאם נותנין לי מאה מנה איני מבדה, מנה יש לי אצל פלוני ואין לי אלא עד
אחד, מנין שלא יצטרף עמו, תלמוד לומר מדבר שקר תרחק, הא ודאי שקורי

Yad Dovid

a. rechilus: Why is the report of Do'eg considered *rechilus* rather than
loshon hora? *Kesef Mishneh* (to *Hilchos De'os* 7:1) explains that Achimelech
had not done anything wrong. He was under the impression that Dovid
was on a mission for King Shaul, since Dovid told him: "The King has
commanded me about something" (I *Shmuel* 21:3). The assistance he gave
to Dovid was in no way intended as rebellion against King Shaul; hence
the information supplied by Do'eg is not classed as *loshon hora*, because it
was not derogatory. However, the information did incite King Shaul to
hate Achimelech and the other *kohanim* of Nov, and therefore is classed as
rechilus. See also *Avodas Hamelech* to *Hilchos De'os* 7:2, s.v. "ומש"ר אבל",
who explains that even though in Shaul's eyes the information was a disparagement of Achimelech, nevertheless it was not *loshon hora* since in
truth he had done nothing wrong.

One could ask: Even though Do'eg's report was not derogatory,
should it not be classed as *loshon hora* because it was an indirect cause of
damage (גְּרָמָא בְּנִזְיקִין — see Overview, para. 28)? The answer is that (as
mentioned in the Overview, note 63), the concept of "indirect cause of
damage" does not apply to *rechilus*.

b. Only one witness: I have only one witness to prove that the money is
owed to me, and I cannot win the case unless I produce two witnesses.

The Gemara goes on to ask: "But surely he is lying, and the Torah says: 'You shall not give false testimony [a] against your fellow!' [ibid 20:13]." Therefore the Gemara concludes: "Rather, the case is where his rebbe tells him: 'Certainly I have one witness. Now you come and just stand there [in the *beis din*] without saying anything; thus you will not be telling a lie.'" That is, [the rebbe simply wants the debtor to think that he has brought two witnesses,] so that he will be afraid and admit the truth. Even so, the student is forbidden to comply, because the Torah says: "Keep far from a falsehood." All the more so concerning the prohibition of *loshon hora*, which is more stringent [than the command to keep far from falsehood] —certainly one is forbidden to obey his rebbe's request [to tell him something, if the report would involve *loshon hora*].

[*Be'er Mayim Chaim* next introduces a new proof of this same law:]

Moreover, the mitzvah of honoring a king [of Israel] is certainly more stringent than that of honoring one's father or rebbe; for even according to those who rule that a rebbe can relinquish his honor, a king cannot do so[b] [*Kiddushin* 32b; *Kesubos* 17a].

Yet even so, the Gemara in *Sanhedrin* [49a] says that if a king (of Israel) commands one to transgress a Torah prohibition, one must not do so. See the Gemara there,[c] which says: "One might think [the requirement to obey the king applies] even to [cancelling study of] the words of the Torah? [To dispel this notion] the verse says: 'Only be strong and take courage.' [And the word] 'only' is an exclusion."

How much the more so, one must not obey the command of one's father or rebbe [if that means transgressing a Torah commandment]!

As for what I wrote in the text [of *Mekor HaChaim*], that [one may not obey one's father or rebbe] even [if obeying him only involves] *avak loshon hora*, this is based on what I proved above [at the beginning of this clause] that if one's father or rebbe commands

קמשקר, ורחמנא אמר לא תענה ברעך עד שקר, אלא כגון דאמר ליה ודאי חד
סהדא אית לי, ותא את קום התם ולא תימא ולא מידי, דהא לא מפקית מפומך
שיקרא, פירוש רק כדי שיתיירא ויודה על האמת, אפילו הכי אסור משום שנאמר
מדבר שקר תרחק. וכל-שכן באיסור לשון הרע החמור מזה שלא יציית לו. ועוד
דבודאי כבוד המלך חמור מכבוד אביו ורבו, וראיה דאפילו למאן דאמר הרב
שמחל על כבודו כבודו מחול, מלך שמחל על כבודו אין כבודו מחול, כדאמרינן
בקדושין ובכתובות (יז ע"א), ואפילו הכי אמרינן בסנהדרין (מ"ט ע"א) דאם
המלך (היינו מלך ישראל) מצוהו לעבור על דברי תורה שלא ישמע לו עי"ש
בגמרא יכול אפילו לדברי תורה תלמוד לומר רק חזק ואמץ, רק מיעוטא הוא,
ועל אחת כמה וכמה דאין צריך לשמוע לאביו ורבו. ומה שכתבתי בפנים דאפילו
לאבק לשון הרע הוא ממה שהוכחתי לעיל דאפילו לעבור על דבריהם אין צריך
לשמוע לאביו ורבו.

Yad Dovid

a. you shall not give false testimony: : Surely if the student testifies as the
second witness he is violating the verse (*Shemos* 20:13) which prohibits
giving false testimony. Why then do we need the verse (ibid. 23:7) about
keeping far from falsehood?

b. Cannot do so: If the king says 'I do not require you to honor me,' one
must still honor him.

c. The Gemara there: The Gemara discusses the story of Amasa, the head
of King Dovid's army. The King commanded him to muster the men of
Yehudah within three days. When Amasa went to do so he found them
just beginning to study a certain tractate of the Gemara. Mustering them
to the army at that point would have meant cancelling their studies.
Amasa reasoned to himself as follows: It is written concerning Yehoshua:
"Anyone who rebels against your commandment and will not listen to
your words in anything that you command him, will be put to death; only
be strong and take courage" (*Yehoshua* 1:18). (The verse is understood to
apply to any king of Israel, not just Yehoshua.) From this one might conclude that one must obey the king even if it entails cessation of Torah
study. However, the verse says: "only be strong and take courage," and
the word "only" is expounded as excluding something. In this case it ex-
cludes obeying the king if that entails cessation of Torah study, or any
other mitzvah.

him to transgress even a Rabbinic commandment,[a] one is forbidden to obey him.

(9) [to *Mekor HaChaim* , clause 5, p. 120] **If they ask him:** I did not mention the simplest case, namely where they ask him to speak *loshon hora* itself; for this is uncommon.

Now, one might think there is another reason why I did not mention this simplest case: namely, that if they ask him to speak *loshon hora* they are removing themselves from the class of "your people"[b] and so it would be obvious that there is no mitzvah to honor them. However, this is not true, for *Sefer Mitzvos Gadol* [positive commandment 112], in discussing the commandment to honor one's father, writes that someone who tells another to transgress a Torah commandment does not thereby remove himself from the class of "your people."[c] The only exception is someone who urges another to worship an idol; such a person, who is termed a מסית "enticer" [to idolatry] is excluded from the class of "your people." (See *Sefer Mitzvos Gadol*, loc. cit.) [Hence if one's father or rebbe urges one to worship an idol, obviously one should not obey him. However, if they urge one to transgress some other prohibition, such as that against speaking *loshon hora*, they nevertheless remain in the class of "your people," and the ruling that one should not obey them is derived from the proofs set forth above, *Be'er Mayim Chaim*, clause 8.]

(10) [to *Mekor HaChaim*, clause 6, p. 122] **Just as with all other negative precepts:** Obviously, since as explained above in the Introduction this negative precept [against speaking *loshon hora*] encompasses many other negative and positive precepts, it is, to say the least, in no way inferior to the other negative precepts in this respect. [That is, if one must give up all his belongings rather than transgress other negative precepts, surely he must do so for this one.] But even without this,[d] the Halachah is that even for a Rabbinic prohibition one is required to give up everything he owns rather than transgress (see *Yoreh De'ah* 157:1, and *Biur HaGra* and *Chiddushei Rabbi Akiva Eger* there. And see below, *Hilchos Rechilus*, ch. 1, *Be'er Mayim Chaim* there, clauses 12 and 13.)

(ט) בקשו ממנו. לא ציירתי בפשיטות כגון אם בקשו ממנו לשון הרע גופא
דזה אינו מצוי. ולא משום דבזה נקרא אביו אינו עושה מעשה עמך ופשיטא
דאינו מחויב לכבדו, דזה אינו, דכבר כתב הסמ"ג במצות עשה של כיבוד אב
דבזה שאדם אומר לחבירו לעשות איסור אינו נקרא אינו עושה מעשה עמך רק
במסית עיין שם.

(י) ככל שאר לאוין. דפשיטא דזה הלאו שכולל בעצמותו עוד הרבה לאוין
ועשין אחרים כמבואר לעיל בפתיחה, לפחות איננו גרוע משאר לאוין אחרים,
ובלאו הכי עיין שם ביו"ד דפסקו דאפילו על איסור דרבנן צריך גם כן ליתן כל
אשר לו ולא לעבור עליהן עי"ש בביאור הגר"א ובחידושי ר' עקיבא איגר ועיין
לקמן בהלכות רכילות כלל א' בבאר מים חיים ס"ק י"ב וי"ג מה שכתבנו שם.

Yad Dovid

a. even a Rabbinic commandment: *Be'er Mayim Chaim* maintains that *avak
loshon hora* is a Rabbinic prohibition.

b. they are removing themselves from the class of "your people:" The
Torah commands: "You shall not curse a leader among your people"
(וְנָשִׂיא בְעַמְּךָ לֹא תָאֹר; *Shemos* 22:27). (*Mechilta* explains that the verse does
not refer only to a "leader," but applies to any Jew.) The Gemara expounds this to mean that one may not curse him as long as he is acting
like one of "your people;" but if he intentionally transgresses any of the
mitzvos incumbent upon the Jewish people and has not repented, then in
this respect he is not in the class of "your people," and there is no obligation to act towards him as the Torah would otherwise require (see
Yevamos 22b). (For more on this topic see below, ch. 4, clause 7.) For example, in the case of a leader who deliberately transgresses a mitzvah, one
who curses him does not violate the above negative precept.

c. does not thereby remove himself: That is, one removes himself from
the class of "your people" by transgressing a mitzvah, but not by telling
others to transgress it.

d. even without this: Even without taking into consideration that the prohibition against *loshon hora* is at least as weighty as other Scriptural prohibitions.

(11) [to *Mekor HaChaim*, clause 7, p. 122] **Certainly it is forbidden:** It was not, God forbid, concerning this type of situation that *Chazal* said [*Kesubos* 17a]: "A person should always strive to be involved with people." [When our sages said this they meant] only if those people do not do forbidden things. But in this case the people are considered wicked, and it is altogether forbidden to join with them in their speaking. And even if they will bear enmity towards him for this, he must not, God forbid, fear that at all, as *Shulchan Aruch* rules in *Yoreh De'ah* [112:15], that one is forbidden to transgress even a Rabbinic commandment for fear of people's enmity — and all the more so a grave prohibition like this [*loshon hora*].

(12) [to *Mekor HaChaim*, clause 8, p. 126] **Or writes the matter about him:** It is obvious that concerning this form [of *loshon hora*] it is written: "Cursed is he who strikes his fellow Jew in secret"[a] [*Devorim* 27:24]. Moreover, the matter is dealt with explicitly in *Sanhedrin* [30a, where the Gemara asks:] "How do we write [the verdict]?"[b] Rabbi Yochanan said [that we simply write:] 'Acquitted' — so as to avoid *rechilus*. And even Resh Lakish[c] agrees with Rabbi Yochanan on the basic law that the sin of *rechilus* can be committed by writing; for he disagrees with Rabbi Yochanan only because it [the verdict stating only "acquitted"] appears like a lie. It follows of course that the same law applies[d] to *loshon hora*.

Yad Dovid

a. who strikes his fellow Jew in secret: The other verses forbidding *loshon hora* (see above, clause 1, *Be'er Mayim Chaim*, clauses 3, 4) might be construed as referring specifically to speech or gestures. But there can be no question that our present verse includes writing.

b. how do we write [the verdict]: The Gemara there deals with a financial case where, by a vote of two judges against one, a litigant is absolved of obligation. The verdict must be handed to the litigant in writing, and the question is how to phrase it. Rabbi Yochanan says that the verdict should simply state: "Acquitted," without specifying how each judge voted. This

(יא) בודאי דאסור. וחס-וחלילה על ענין כזה לא אמרו חז"ל לעולם תהא דעתו
של אדם מעורבת עם הבריות, דדוקא אם הם בריות שאין עושין דבר איסור,
אבל בזה רשעים מיקרי ואסור להתחבר עמהם כלל בספוריהם. ואפילו אם יהיה
להם עליו איבה איבה עבור זה אין לו חס ושלום לחוש כלל לזה, כמו שנפסק ביורה
דעה בסימן קי"ב סט"ו דאפילו לעבור על איסור דרבנן אסור משום איבה, ועל
אחת כמה וכמה באיסור חמור כזה.

(יב) כותב עליו דבר זה. פשוט הוא דבכי האי גוונא כתיב ארור מכה רעהו
בסתר, ועוד גמרא מפורשת היא בסנהדרין (ל ע"א) מכתב היכי כתבי רבי יוחנן
אומר זכאי משום לא תלך רכיל, ואפילו ריש לקיש גם-כן מודה לו בעצם הדין
דבכתיבה שייך רכילות דלא קפליג עליה רק משום דמיחזי כשיקרא וממילא הוא
הדין בלשון הרע דינא הכי.

Yad Dovid

is to avoid creating animosity towards the judge who voted to obligate the
litigant. (Creating such animosity would be *rechilus*.)

c. even Resh Lakish: Resh Lakish maintains that in the written verdict the
litigant should be given the names of the judges and how each one voted,
for if they simply write "acquitted," without specifying how each judge
voted, it might seem like a lie (i.e. it would appear as if the court is trying
to give the false impression that all three judges voted for acquittal). In
fact, Resh Lakish maintains that in this case, informing the litigant that a
judge voted against him is not *rechilus* (*Tosafos* there, s.v. "משום"), because the litigant will assume that in the end even the dissenting judge
agreed with the other two (see *Hilchos Rechilus*, ch. 1, *Be'er Mayim Chaim*,
clause 14). However, Resh Lakish agrees that it is forbidden to transmit
rechilus by writing. (Otherwise the Gemara certainly would have said that
this itself is the basis of their disagreement, and the question of appearing
to lie would be irrelevant.)

d. the same law applies: I.e., the prohibition of *loshon hora*, like that of
rechilus, can be violated by writing.

Be'er Mayim Chaim   Chapter 1

(13) [to *Mekor HaChaim*, clause 8, p. 126] **By way of hint or gesture:** [How do we know that if one conveys the derogatory information by hint or gesture alone, this still constitutes *loshon hora*?] This is clear from the commentary of *Rashi* to the verse in *Parashas Kedoshim*: "You shall not go about as a talebearer among your people" (*Vayikra* 19:16). Based on the translation of Onkelos, *Rashi* explains that this verse refers to winking the eyes — "for this is the way of all talebearers, to wink with their eyes and hint their words of incitement, so that the other listeners [i.e. bystanders] should not understand."[a] This too is the plain meaning of the verse in *Mishlei* (6:12-13): "An unscrupulous person, a man of sin, goes with twisted mouth; he winks with his eyes, scrapes with his feet, points with his fingers."

Do not suppose that what we have just written is contradicted by the Gemara in *Berachos* [8a] which states that in the West [i.e. Eretz Israel] when a man married a woman they would ask him: "found" or "find?" where "found" refers to the verse in *Mishlei* [18:22]: "He who has found a wife has found good, " while "find" refers to *Koheles* [7:26]: "But I find the woman more bitter than death."[b] [Now, how could such a custom be permissible?] Surely *loshon hora* is forbidden even if conveyed by hint, and even if the information conveyed is true, as long as there is no constructive purpose[c] in conveying it! And [if one were to think that in this case the derogatory hint is permitted because it concerns his own wife, this is not so, for] it is forbidden to speak *loshon hora* about one's wife (see below, ch. 8) just as about anyone else. [How, then, could the Gemara permit the bridegroom to reply: "Find?"]

It would seem [that the answer is] in accord with what *Rambam* writes [*Hilchos De'os* 7:5], that if a matter has already been made known[d] in the presence of at least three people [together in one sitting - בְּאַפֵּי תְלָתָא] one who repeats it afterwards is not in violation of the prohibition against *loshon hora*, as long as he did not intend to spread the information and make it more known.[e] In light of this, one could explain simply that in most cases if the woman is so

162

(יג) בדרך רמז. כן מוכח ברש"י בחומש פרשת קדושים בפסוק לא תלך רכיל
בעמיך על מה שתרגם אונקלוס בלשון קורצין פירש רש"י לשון קורץ בעיניו
שכן דרך כל הולכי רכיל לקרוץ בעיניהם ולרמז דברי רכילותן שלא יבינו שאר
השומעים עכ"ל וכן מוכח פשטיה דקרא במשלי (ו' פסוק י"ב) אדם בליעל איש
און וגו' קורץ בעיניו מולל ברגליו מורה באצבעותיו.

ולא תקשה על זה ממה שאמרו בברכות (ח ע"א) במערבא כי נסיב איניש
איתתא אמרי ליה הכי מצא מצא או מוצא, מצא דכתיב מצא אשה מצא טוב, ומוצא
דכתיב ומוצא אני מר ממות את האשה, הלא לשון הרע אסור אפילו בדרך רמז
ואסור אפילו על אמת כל שאין מזה מזה תועלת על להבא כדלקמן בכלל י' בסופו
ואין נפקא מינה באיסור לשון הרע בין אשתו ואחר כדלקמן בכלל ח'. ונראה
לפי מה שכתב הרמב"ם דדבר שנתפרסם כבר באפי תלתא המספר אחר כך אין
בו משום לשון הרע אך שלא יתכוין להעביר הקול ולגלותו יותר. אם כן נוכל
לומר בפשיטות, דרגילות הוא דאשה רעה שנוכל לומר עליה שהיא מר ממות,
נתפרסם בוודאי מכבר עניניה באפי תלתא לפחות, ואם-כן הבעל שמספר אחר
כך ענין רעתה ואינו מתכוין להעביר הקול אין עובר על זה משום איסור לשון
הרע.

Yad Dovid

a. so that the other listeners [i.e. bystanders] should not understand: The
talebearer wishes to transmit his *rechilus* in secret to one particular listener.

b. more bitter than death: If the bridegroom replied: "Find," he would be
hinting that his bride was an evil wife. Since the Gemara cites this custom
without condemning it, we might conclude that one is permitted to con-
vey *loshon hora* by means of a hint.

c. constructive purpose:: See below, ch. 10, clauses 13-14.

d. already been made known: This intricate subject is explained at length
below, ch. 2; the permission does not apply unless many conditions are
fulfilled.

e. to spread the information and make it more known: See Overview,
para. 23.

163

evil that she fits the description "more bitter than death," certainly her defects have already become known to at least three people.[a] Hence when the husband afterwards tells someone about her badness, without intending to spread the information, he is not in violation[b] of the prohibition against *loshon hora*.

This foregoing answer would also explain the Gemara in *Yevamos* [63b] where Rav[c] was teaching his son the verse, "But I find the woman more bitter than death." His son asked him for an example, to which he replied: "For example, your mother."

This latter passage could also be explained another way: In this incident the son already knew his mother's character, but in learning the verse he asked for an example because he wanted to understand how bad a woman's character has to be in order to fit the description, "more bitter than death." It was only in order to answer this question that the father replied: "For example, your mother." Thus it is clear that his intent was only to explain the verse, not to deprecate his wife. This is in the category of accurate derogatory information spoken for a constructive purpose; and such speech is permitted,[d] as explained below, ch. 10.

(14) [to *Mekor HaChaim*, clause 8, p. 126] **In all forms:** This means even if one does not speak or write [the derogatory information] about the person, but only shows letters that the person wrote to him, where it is noticeable from the letters' contents that the person is not wise or learned; or similar kinds of disparagement. This too is included in the prohibition against *loshon hora*[e] And even though this needs no proof, nevertheless I shall show you that this kind of *loshon hora* is also mentioned by the Torah as forbidden; for we

Yad Dovid

a. to at least three people: If her bad character was known, why did her husband marry her? The answer is that it may not have been so well publicized that her husband knew about it before the marriage; for (as implied below , ch. 2, *Mekor HaChaim*, clause 4, s.v. ("הדבר נתפרסם שככבר לא אם"

וכן מה שאמרו ביבמות (סג ע"ב) אמר ליה חייא ב"ר לרב כתיב ומוצא אני מר
ממות את האשה כגון מאן, אמר ליה כגון אמך, גם-כן ניחא בתירוץ זה. ובזה יש
לומר עוד באופן אחר, דשם שחייא ב"ר ידע את טבע אמו, אך שאל כגון מאן
פירוש עד היכן נקרא אשה רעה, והשיב כגון אמך, מוכח הוא שכוונתו למיסבר
קראי ולא לגנותה בזה, וזה דומה למי שמכוין לתועלת בדבר שהוא אמת
וכדלקמן בכלל י'.

(יד) בכל גווני. פירוש אפילו אם אין מדבר או כותב עליו, רק שמראה לאחרים
מכתביו שכתב פלוני אליו, שניכר מכותלי מכתביו שאיננו חכם או למדן וכדומה
מעניני גנות, גם זה בכלל איסור לשון הרע הוא. ואף שאין זה צריך ראיה,
אעפ"כ אראה לך שגם מין לשה"ר זה נזכר בתורה לאיסור, שבפסוק וגם אתה
ידעת את אשר עשה לי יואב בן צרויה וגו' פירשו רז"ל (במד"ר פכ"ג)

Yad Dovid

the situation of בְּאַפֵּי תְלָתָא "in the presence of three people," is a stage
before that of "a well-known matter" (דָבָר מְפוּרְסָם). Only in the latter
stage is the information so widespread that it may be assumed everyone
knows about it. This concept of "a well-known matter" is discussed in the
Overview, sect.7.

b. not in violation: For further discussion of this question: "found" or
"find?" which they asked in *Eretz Yisroel*, see *Ikrei Dinim*, ch. 2, footnote 6;
and *Nesivos Chaim* to this clause of *Be'er Mayim Chaim*.

c. Rav: Our Gemara reads: Rav Yehudah.

d. and such speech is permitted: One may use another's misconduct to
explain a point of Torah to someone who is already aware of this person's
behavior. This is considered a constructive purpose. The person spoken
about suffers no further degradation as a result of the utterance, and the
sole intent of the speaker is to elucidate a point of Torah, not to discuss
needlessly the misdeeds of the person (*Sefer Hilchos Loshon Hora U'rechilus*,
p. 33).

e. included in the prohibition against loshon hora: The point is
that even though he does not reveal his *loshon hora* by means of
speech, hint or gesture, but only by way of his action (e.g., showing

read [in *I Kings* 2:5 that King Dovid on his deathbed instructed his son Shlomo to mete out punishment to certain people who had harmed Dovid. One of these was Yoav, regarding whom Dovid told Shlomo:] "You also know what Yoav ben Tzeruyah did to me." Our Sages[a] of blessed memory, explain what Yoav did to Dovid: He showed the Sanhedrin the letter Dovid had sent him,[b] ordering him to place Uriah in a position on the battlefront where the fighting was most fierce (and therefore he would be killed). Yoav's intent in showing this to the Sanhedrin was to lessen their esteem for Dovid.

(15) [to *Mekor HaChaim*, clause 9, p. 128] **He also attributes the selfsame defect to himself and even if he begins by disparaging himself first:** [This law can be derived] from what we find concerning the Prophet Yeshayahu, who said: "Woe is me, for I am destroyed, for I am a man of contaminated lips, and I dwell among a people of contaminated lips!" (*Yeshayahu* 6:5). Now, Yeshayahu did not intend, Heaven forbid, to disparage the Jewish People. He was only expressing his distress concerning his own dangerous situation, saying: "Woe is me, for I am destroyed," which meant, as explained by *Rashi* and other commentators: 'Behold, I shall die, for I am not worthy — neither based on my own deeds nor on my ancestors' deeds[c] — of seeing the Divine Presence'. Moreover, he first deprecated himself, saying: "...for I am a man of contaminated lips." Nevertheless he was punished for this, as it is written [ibid., v. 6-7]: "Then one of the angels flew to me and in his hand there was a live coal [and he touched it to my mouth]." And the Sages say[d] that the Holy One, Blessed is He [when sending the angel with

Y a d   D o v i d

letters), nevertheless he is considered a "talebearer" (*Nesivos Chaim, Shevilei Chaim*, clause 18).

a. **our Sages:** *Rashi*, citing *Tanchuma, Parashas Masei* 9; see also *Bamidbar Rabbah* 23:13.

שהראה לסנהדרין את המכתב ששלח לו דוד שיעמיד את אוריה בעת חזקת
המלחמה כדי שיתמעט עי"ז מדרגת דוד בעיניהם.

(טו) גינה את עצמו וכו'. ואפילו הקדים וכו'. ממה שמצינו בישעיה כשאמר
אוי לי כי נדמיתי כי איש טמא שפתים אנכי ובתוך עם טמא שפתים אנכי יושב.
ואף שישעיה לא כיון חס ושלום לגנות בזה את ישראל, רק היה מתאונן על
עצמו ואומר אוי לי כי נדמיתי וגו' וביארו כמו שפירש רש"י והמפרשים הריני
מת שלא הייתי כדאי שאראה פני השכינה לא מצד מעשי ולא מצד מעשה
אבותי, וגם הקדים לבזות לעצמו וכמו שאמר כי איש וגו', ואפילו הכי נענש
על-זה כמו שכתוב שם ויעף אלי וגו' ובידו רצפה. ואמרו חז"ל (שהש"ר פ"א)

Yad Dovid

b. the letter Dovid had sent him: See *II Shmuel* 11:15. (If showing the letter had not been prohibited, Dovid would not have instructed that Yoav
be punished for it.)

c. neither based on my own deeds nor on my ancestors' deeds: Clearly
the purpose of his statement was to explain the danger of his own situation, and his words about the nation of Israel were only incidental to this.

d. the sages say: *Yalkut Shimoni*, part 2, *remez* 406; *Midrash Rabbah, Shir
Hashirim, parashah* 1, sub-clause 6.

167

the coal] said: "Crush the mouth[a] that spoke *loshon hora* about My children." *Yalkut Shimoni* there adds that in reply to Yeshayahu's statement, "I am a man of contaminated lips, and I dwell among a people of contaminated lips," the Holy One, Blessed is He said: "You are allowed to say this about yourself, [b] but you are not allowed[c] to say it about them."

Yad Dovid

a. crush the mouth: רְצוֹץ פֶּה, a play on the word רְצָפָה ("live coal").

b. about yourself: We have no clear proof from here that one may speak *loshon hora* to others about himself, for in this case *Yeshayahu* was speaking in private, before Hashem alone; hence it was not *loshon hora*, since everything is revealed and known to Hashem; rather it was like a confession to Hashem. Why, then, did Hashem reprimand the prophet for mentioning the sins of the Jewish people? Only because He does not want us to speak *loshon hora* about others to Him. (This is clear in *Midrash Rabbah* here, which says: "A servant should not speak *loshon hora* to his master.") On the other hand, if we speak disparagingly about ourselves to Him, it is only like confession, not *loshon hora* (*Ali Be'er* to *Be'er Mayim Chaim* here; for a lengthy discussion of this subject see *Ali Be'er* loc. cit.; see also *Marpeh Loshon*, pamphlet 3, p. 23).

c. you are not allowed: You are forbidden to speak *loshon hora* about others, even if you begin by speaking the same *loshon hora* about yourself.

168

שאמר לו הקדוש ברוך הוא למלאך רצוץ פה שאמר דילטוריא על בני. וגם על
שאמר כי איש וגו' השיבו הקב"ה עליך אתה רשאי לומר ואי אתה רשאי לומר
עליהם וכמו דאיתא בילקוט שם.

SUBJECT INDEX

A

abuse (possible abuse of their work), 90

alarm (caused by speech), 37, para 28

Amasa
    (disobeyed king in order to avoid sinning), 157 "c"

avak loshon hora
    caused by someone's request for information, 120
    definition of, 31, sec 6
    difference between it and gesturing, 127 "b"
    forbidden Rabbinically, 158; 159 "a"

avak rechilus (definition of), 27, sec 2

awareness of sin (benefits of), 106

B

baalei loshon hora
    definition of, 116 "a"
    lose share in world to come, 118
    severity of their sin, 116
    staying out of their category, 100

beis din
    emissary insulted, 132
    written verdict of, 160

believing
    loshon hora, 31 para 21
    rechilus , 26 para 7

bridegroom (hinting "found" or "find"),162

intent to disparage, 30 para 19

interesting information (not considered constructive purpose), 46 para 53, 126 "a"

J

Jew (*loshon hora* specifically about), 112 "b"

judge (may not relate: "I voted for acquittal"), 138

K

king
  disobeying him to avoid *loshon hora*, 156

  honoring him, 152-154

King Dovid (his letter displayed to disparage him), 166

King Shaul (episode of Do'eg), 152

L

leprosy (punishment for speaking loshon hora), 31 ftnt 35; 116 "b"

letter
  displayed to disparage the writer, 126; 164
  prohibition of writing *loshon hora* in, 126; 160

life (not required to sacrifice one's life), 118 "a"; 153 "d"

limbs (248 spiritual limbs), 52

livelihood (giving it up to avoid *loshon hora*), 120

loshon hora
  about a Jew or a non-Jew, 112 "b"
  about oneself, 128; 166; 138 "b"
  as main cause of exile, 60-62
  believing it, 31 para 21
  conveyed by gesture, 126; 162
  conveyed by letter, 126
  definition of, 27, 37 sec 3, 8
  derivation of the prohibition, 28 sec. 4; 140
  equivalent to cardinal sins, 118; 118 "a"; 150 "a"
  explaining a verse by means of, 154; 165 "d"
  habitually speaking, 114-116

in newspapers, 126 "a"
leprosy as punishment for, 31 ftnt 35; 116 "b"
listening to, 31 para 21
more severe than cardinal sins, 150
more severe than *rechilus* — or vice versa, 140
occasionally speaking, 114
prevents blessings, 64
prevents prayer from being heard, 70
reasons why people transgress, 72ff
strengthens heavenly accusers, 66
true information is *loshon hora* 112; 132-136; 162

lying, see "falsehood"

M

merits lost by speaking *loshon hora*, 116 "b"

Miriam punished for *loshon hora*, B142

mitzvos performed through suffering, 124

monetary loss to avoid *loshon hora*, 120; 118 "a"; 158

Moshe (in episode of Dosan and Aviram), 132

motzi shem ra
    definition of, 47 sec 15
    more severe than *loshon hora*, 47 para. 56;164; 138
    punishable by death at the hands of heaven, 114 "c"
    through just one untrue word, 136

N

Need for a work on *loshon hora*, 80

negation of people's qualities, 29 para 18, 38

newspapers (*rechilus and loshon hora* in), 126 "a"

non-Jew (*loshon hora* about a), 112 "b"

O

occasional loshon hora compared to habitual *loshon hora*, 114
    punishable by leprosy, 116 "b"

INDEX OF HEBREW TERMS

WORKS CITED BY *YAD DOVID*

1) *Ali Be'er* , Rabbi S. Rosner (Jerusalem, 5750/(1990).

2) *Chelkas Binyomin*, Rabbi B. Cohen (Brooklyn, N.Y., 5753/1993).

3) *Hilchos Loshon Hora U'Rechilus*, Rabbi Y. K. Krohn (Chevrah Shmiras Haloshon, Lakewood).

4) *Ikrei Dinim*, Rabbi S. Houminer, *z'tzl* (Jerusalem; printed in most early editions of *Sefer Chofetz Chaim*).

5) *Kitzur Hilchos Loshon Hora* R. C. Freiman, (Shivuk VeYetzu, Bnei Brak, 5753/1993).

6) *Loshon Chaim*, Rabbi B. Eisenblatt (Jerusalem, 5738/1978).

7) *Marpeh Loshon* (ongoing series of pamphlets; *Va'ad Lema'an Shmiras Haloshon*, Jerusalem).

8) *Mateh Yechiel*, R. E. Shlesinger (Bnei Brak).

9) *Nesivos Chaim* , Rabbi M. Kaufmann (Bnei Brak, 5751/1991).

10) *Ohev Yammim*, Rabbi S. Hulas (Jerusalem, Machon Be'er Heitev, 5751/1991).

11) *Oz Nidbru*, R. B. Zilber (Bnei Brak).

12) Responsa *LeChofetz BeChaim*, Rabbi S. Rosner (Jerusalem, 1996).

13) *Zeh HaShulchan*, Rabbi Y. Deblitzky (Bnei Brak).

Approbation of R' Chaim P. Scheinberg

6 Adar 5754

I hereby comply with the pure-hearted request of an outstanding, God-fearing Torah scholar, R' Dovid Marchant, *shlita*, who is already known among Israel for his previous books, *Understanding Shemittah* (Engl.) and השאיפה לגדולה. He has now shown me some pages from his new book, an English translation of that holy and wonderful work, *Chofetz Chaim, Hilchos Loshon Hora and Rechilus*. His translation includes an extensive, clear and detailed commentary not only on *Mekor HaChaim* but also on *Be'er Mayim Chaim*. One can clearly recognize that he has labored greatly with the labor of Torah to clarify the Talmudic sources cited in *Be'er Mayim Chaim*, as well as the profound analysis of those passages presented by *Chofetz Chaim*. In addition, R' Marchant has occupied himself very diligently in mastering the subject, especially through close interaction with other scholars; for he has discussed and debated the topics with outstanding experts specializing in this matter. Moreover, while living in Gateshead he merited to give classes to *bnei Torah* on the laws of *loshon hora* and on the text of *Sefer Chofetz Chaim*. This book is very much needed, especially in our days. Our Sages, of blessed memory, said (*Yoma* 9) that because of groundless hatred the Temple was destroyed and we were exiled from our land; and *Chofetz Chaim*, זצ"ל, explains in his Introduction that the intent of this dictum was to *loshon hora* as well; for *loshon hora* is a product of hatred; otherwise, the punishment would not have been so great. And, as the holy *Chofetz Chaim* discusses at length in his Introduction: So long as we do not see to it that this sin is remedied, how can the Redemption come?

Moreover, in our day we have seen a great awakening of interest in these laws. Therefore, we must express our appreciation to HaRav HaGaon, R' Marchant, who has taken this holy task upon himself, the work of Heaven, and who has merited the help of Heaven in writing this book. And I was very happy to see the fruits of his efforts to enable the English speaking public to merit the study of this extraordinary topic. He has achieved a great accomplishment in opening up that which was closed for these people who are thirsty to study and understand the holy words of *Chofetz Chaim* זצ"ל , and this basic, essential work of his. R' Marchant has set it before them like a *shulchan aruch*, a well-laid table, in a clear, easily understood style. Undoubtedly it will be of great advantage in enabling people to know the laws of *loshon hora* and related laws, and how to fulfull these laws in practice. And every individual is obligated to study these laws, for without persistent study of them it is almost impossible not to transgress them. Therefore, we express our thanks to the author for his good deed, and wish him success in carrying out the desire of Hashem. When one brings merit to the public, the merit of the public is attributed to him. May we all merit to see the fulfillment of the prophetic promise that the whole earth will be full of the knowledge of Hahem, with the coming of our righteous Redeemer quickly, in our time, Amen.

For the sake of the Torah and those who study it.

Chaim Pinchas Scheinberg

Approbation of R' Moishe Sternbuch

Erev Rosh Chodesh Tammuz, 5757

To: The honorable R' Dovid Marchant, *shlita* :

I have read your book on the laws of *loshon hora*, based on the classic *Sefer Chofetz Chaim*, with your commentary, *Yad Dovid*, [and have found that] everything is written in clear easily understood English.

As is known, *loshon hora* is one of the weightiest prohibitions in the Torah, and only through study of the relevant laws is it possible to avoid this transgression; and now, with your book, you have opened a gateway for the English-speaking public to study these laws and to understand the aspects of the prohibition.

The main remedy for having spoken *loshon hora* is to sanctify one's speech from now on. Thus, even if one has not been careful about it in the past, the door is open to him [to rectify the matter]; and precisely with such a commonly violated prohibition, if a person sanctifies himself and is careful about it, his reward is all the greater. My teacher, the Gaon R' M. Shneider, זצ"ל, told me that he once heard someone ask the *Chofetz Chaim*, זצ"ל, in person why he had not cited and emphasized the words of *Rambam* (*Hilchos Teshuvah* 3:6), who writes: "And these are the ones who have no portion in the world to come, but who are cut off and destroyed and punished for all eternity for the magnitude of their wickedness and sin: the apostates, the non-believers, those who deny the Torah, those who deny the Resurrection of the Dead and the coming of the Redeemer ... murderers, those who are habituated to *loshon hora*, and those who repudiate their circumcision." From this we see that those who speak *loshon hora* are in the same category as apostates,

183

non-believers, and murderers, who are punished for all eternity. The *Chofetz Chaim* replied: "I did not want to drop such a bomb." [My teacher] explained what he meant: If people were to think that they are in the same category as apostates who are liable to eternal punishment, they would think they have no remedy, and would not repent; therefore the *Chofetz Chaim* chose not to cite the passage. And the truth is that there is a remedy for this — namely, to accept upon oneself to be careful about this transgression from now on. (And in Ch. 7 of *Hilchos De'os*, *Rambam* writes that speaking *loshon hora* is comparable to denying the existence of God.)

Now, that large segment of the Jewish People who are English speaking will find the laws set forth in your book; and based on what I have seen, it is understandable to all. Likewise, the *Bnei Torah* will find the style clear and easily understood, enabling them to review the laws.

I hope that, with the help of Heaven, the schools will utilize your book to establish regular lessons and tests, for when people are trained from their youth it is easier for them to be careful about the laws. We are obligated to train our youth in all the mitzvos and prohibitions, and, all the more so, in avoiding the prohibitions of *loshon hora* and *rechilus*.

Chazal said: "Study leads to observance." The Holy Temple was destroyed because of groundless hatred, which is the source of *loshon hora*, and when we repair the underlying cause, then the Holy One, Blessed is He, will hasten and speed our Redemption. *Chazal* say that if a person is negligent about the prohibition of *loshon hora*, it is forbidden to be his neighbor (see *Rambam, Hilchos De'os* 7:6); and on the other hand, when one remedies this transgression he makes peace above and below.

Thus I happily add my blessing that this book will be widely studied and will distinguish itself among the House of Israel; and may the Holy One, Blessed is He, hasten and speed our Redemption and the rescue of our souls.

Eagerly awaiting the abundant mercy of Heaven,

Moishe Sternbuch

Approbation of HaRav HaGaon, R' Betzalel Rakow, shlita, Rav of Gateshead

Our friend, the outstanding Rav, great in Torah and fear of Heaven, R' David Marchant, *shlita*, has sent me some pages of his book, an English translation of *Mekor HaChaim*, and *Be'er Mayim Chaim* with his commentary, *Yad Dovid*, which he wishes to publish in order to increase the merits of the public and to save them from the severe prohibition of *loshon hora*.

In truth, I need not explain at length why books of this kind are so greatly needed, for the matter is already well known. Therefore, I only wish to testify about the author, *shlita*, for I know the great effort and labor that he has invested in the study of the works of *Chofetz Chaim*, and I know that he practices these laws as excellently as he teaches them.

As is well known, *Chofetz Chaim*, זצוקללה"ה, received an approbation of his work, *Shemiras Haloshon* from the mighty *Gaon* of Nikoli, one of the great men of that generation, R' Ben-Zion of Belsk, זצ"ל, only after the latter had investigated the *Chofetz Chaim* for a full week to find out if he practiced the laws as excellently as he taught them.

Hence I extend my best wishes to my friend, the author, that he should successfully complete the publication of his work and thereby increase the merits of the people.

And on this merit may we be worthy of complete redemption soon.

In honor of all who labor in the Torah, and in honor of the author, *shlita* --

Betzalel Rakow

2 Elul 5757

To the outstanding Rav and well-known author, R' Dovid Marchant, *shlita:*

I have received sample pages of your important book, an English translation of *Sefer Chofetz Chaim,* in which both *Mekor HaChaim* and *Be'er Mayim Chaim* are translated, with wonderful elaborations and explications worthwhile to all. It is apparent that you have invested much work and effort to produce this fine pearl, and to examine and clarify a number of topics. Most of your commentary has already been tested and refined by being presented in your public classes and discussed with Torah scholars.

It would be superfluous for me to speak about the importance of guarding speech, which, according to *Ramban,* is a mitzvah incumbent upon us at every moment; and to remember what happened to Miriam; and you have accomplished a great thing with your translation and commentary, for this will make it easier for the public to study these laws, and through study they will remember not to transgress.

Just recently it became known to me, through outreach (*kiruv*) institutions that through this mitzvah of refraining from forbidden types of speech, a number of our non-religious brothers have been brought back to Torah and mitzvos. This book will provide opportunity to help others return.

May you be blessed that through you *Bnei Yisroel* will drink plentifully of the living waters, and may you merit to be counted among those whose righteousness is eternal because they bring merit to the public.

With a blessing of *kesivah uchesimah tovah,*

Shmuel Kamenetzky